WHICH MARY?

Society of Biblical Literature

Symposium Series

Christopher R. Matthews,
Editor

Number 19

WHICH MARY?
The Marys of Early Christian Tradition

WHICH MARY?

The Marys of Early Christian Tradition

Edited by
F. Stanley Jones

Society of Biblical Literature
Atlanta

WHICH MARY?

The Marys of Early Christian Tradition

Library of Congress Cataloging-in-Publication Data

Which Mary? : the Marys of early Christian tradition / edited by F. Stanley Jones.
      p. cm. — (Society of Biblical Literature symposium series ; no. 19)
   Includes bibliographical references and indexes.
   ISBN 1-58983-043-1 (pbk. : alk. paper)
   1. Mary Magdalene, Saint—Congresses. 2. Mary, Blessed Virgin, Saint—Congresses.
I. Jones, F. Stanley. II. Series: Symposium series (Society of Biblical Literature) ; no. 19.
   BS2485 .W45 2002
   232.91--dc21
                                          2002011757

10 09 08 07 06 05 04 03 02   5 4 3 2 1

Printed in the United States of America
on acid-free paper

CONTENTS

ABBREVIATIONS

Primary Sources

Acts Phil.	*Acts of Philip*
Acts Phil. Mart.	*Martyrdom of Philip*
Ascen. Isa.	*Ascension of Isaiah*
Clement of Alexandria	
Strom.	*Stromateis*
Const. ap.	*Constitutiones apostolicae*
Didymus the Blind	
Comm. Eccl.	*Commentarii in Ecclesiasten*
Epiphanius	
Pan.	*Panarion (Adversus haereses)*
Eusebius	
Dem. ev.	*Demonstratio evangelica*
Ecl. proph.	*Eclogae propheticae*
Hist. eccl.	*Historia ecclesiastica*
Gos. Bart.	*Gospel of Bartholomew*
Gos. Mary	*Gospel of Mary*
Gos. Naz.	*Gospel of the Nazarenes*
Gos. Pet.	*Gospel of Peter*
Gos. Phil.	*Gospel of Philip*
Gos. Thom.	*Gospel of Thomas*
Hippolytus	
Haer.	*Refutatio omnium haeresium*
Ignatius (Ign.)	
Eph.	*To the Ephesians*
Smyrn.	*To the Smyrnaeans*
Trall.	*To the Trallians*
Irenaeus	
Haer.	*Adversus haereses*
Jerome	
Helv.	*Adversus Helvidium de Mariae virginitate perpetua*
Josephus	
War	*Jewish War*
Justin Martyr	
Dial.	*Dialogus cum Tryphone*

Origen
 Cels.   *Contra Celsum*
Philo
 Agr.   *De agricultura*
 Contempl.   *De vita contemplativa*
 Leg.   *Legum allegoriae*
Pindar
 Nem.   *Nemeonikai*
Plato
 Prot.   *Protagoras*
 Resp.   *Respublica*
P.Bod.   Bodmer papyri
P.Oxy.   Oxyrhynchus papyri
Prot. Jas.   *Protevangelium of James*
1QS   *Rule of the Community*
T. Adam   *Testament of Adam*

Secondary Sources

ABD	*Anchor Bible Dictionary.* Edited by D. N. Freedman. 6 vols. New York: Doubleday, 1992.
AIRF	Acta instituti romani Finlandiae
AnBoll	*Analecta Bollandiana*
APF	*Archiv für Papyrusforschung*
ASP	American Studies in Papyrology
BASP	*Bulletin of the American Society of Papyrologists*
BCNH.T	Bibliothèque copte de Nag Hammadi, Section "Textes"
BETL	Bibliotheca ephemeridum theologicarum lovaniensium
BRev	*Bible Review*
CBM	Chester Beatty Monographs
CBiPa	Cahiers de biblia patristica
CCSA	Corpus Christianorum series apocryphorum
CNS	*Cristianesimo nella storia*
CSCO	Corpus scriptorum christianorum orientalium
CSCO.Ae	Corpus scriptorum christianorum orientalium: Scriptores aethiopici
CSCO.Sub	Corpus scriptorum christianorum orientalium: Subsidia
CurBS	*Currents in Research: Biblical Studies*
DNP	*Der neue Pauly: Enzyklopädie der Antike.* Edited by H. Cancik and H. Schneider. Stuttgart: Metzler, 1996–.
DRev	*Downside Review*
EKKNT	Evangelisch-katholischer Kommentar zum Neuen Testament
EvT	*Evangelische Theologie*

FRLANT	Forschungen zur Religion und Literatur des Alten und Neuen Testaments
GCS	Die griechische christliche Schriftsteller der ersten [drei] Jahrhunderte
Hen	*Henoch*
Hor	*Horizons*
HSM	Harvard Semitic Monographs
JAC.E	Jahrbuch für Antike und Christentum, Ergänzungsband
JBL	*Journal of Biblical Literature*
JECS	*Journal of Early Christian Studies*
JFSR	*Journal of Feminist Studies in Religion*
JSJSup	Supplements to the Journal for the Study of Judaism
JSOTSup	Journal for the Study of the Old Testament Supplement Series
JSPSup	Journal for the Study of the Pseudepigrapha Supplement Series
JTS	*Journal of Theological Studies*
Leš	*Lešonénu*
Mus	*Muséon: Revue d'études orientales*
NHC	Nag Hammadi Codices
NHL	*Nag Hammadi Library in English*. Edited by J. M. Robinson. 4th rev. ed. Leiden: Brill, 1996.
NHS	Nag Hammadi Studies
NovT	*Novum Testamentum*
NovTSup	Supplements to Novum Testamentum
NRSV	New Revised Standard Version
NTAbh	Neutestamentliche Abhandlungen
NTOA	Novum testamentum et orbis antiquum
NTS	*New Testament Studies*
OrChr	*Oriens christianus*
OTP	*Old Testament Pseudepigrapha*. Edited by J. H. Charlesworth. 2 vols. New York: Doubleday, 1983–85.
PETSE	Papers of the Estonian Theological Society in Exile
PG	Patrologia graeca [Patrologiae cursus completus: Series graeca]. Edited by J.-P. Migne. 162 vols. Paris: Migne, 1857–86.
PL	Patrologia latina [Patrologiae cursus completus: Series latina]. Edited by J.-P. Migne. 217 vols. Paris: Migne, 1844–64.
PO	Patrologia orientalis
PTA	Papyrologische Texte und Abhandlungen
PTMS	Pittsburgh Theological Monograph Series
PTS	Patristische Texte und Studien

PW	Pauly, A. F. *Paulys Realencyclopädie der classischen Alter-tumswissenschaft.* New edition. G. Wissowa. 49 vols. Munich: Druckenmüller, 1894–1980.
RB	*Revue biblique*
REByz	*Revue des études byzantines*
RTP	*Revue de théologie et de philosophie*
SAC	Studies in Antiquity and Christianity
SBLSP	Society of Biblical Literature Seminar Papers
SC	Sources chrétiennes. Paris: Cerf, 1943–.
SHG	Subsidia hagiographica
SHR	Studies in the History of Religions
SHT	Studies in Historical Theology
SPAW.PH	*Sitzungsberichte der Preußischen Akademie der Wissen-schaften: Philosophisch-historische Klasse*
SPMed	Studia patristica mediolanensia
STAT	Suomalaisen Tiedeakatemian toimituksia
StPatr	*Studia patristica*
TDSA	Testi e documenti per lo studio dell'antichità
ThH	Théologie historique
TRSR	Testi e ricerche di scienze religiose
TS	*Theological Studies*
TSK	*Theologische Studien und Kritiken*
TU	Texte und Untersuchungen
WUNT	Wissenschaftliche Untersuchungen zum Neuen Testament
ZKT	*Zeitschrift für katholische Theologie*
ZNW	*Zeitschrift für die neutestamentliche Wissenschaft und die Kunde der älteren Kirche*

Introduction

F. Stanley Jones
California State University, Long Beach

This volume recaptures a session on early Christian Marys sponsored by the Christian Apocrypha Section at the 2000 Annual Meeting of the Society of Biblical Literature. The contributors present the results of their specializations as refined in years of academic labor. Their papers are thus truly appreciable only in written form, as was immediately recognized by Christopher Matthews, who initially suggested inclusion in Symposium. Before comments on why these essays have been assembled and how they relate to each other, a few words are in order about how these cutting-edge contributions generally fit into the vibrant field of New Testament studies.

At the end of the nineteenth century, the "History of Religions School" raised an academic demand: in order to understand the development of early Christianity, New Testament scholars must master not only the canonical writings but all early Christian writings from the same time period, that is, through the middle of the second century at the very least. After an initial spurt of activity, the field seemed somewhat slow in following up on this academically argued demand. In the second half of the twentieth century, however, archaeological discoveries of lost early Christian texts started to mount. The question of the relationship of these texts to the canonical writings proved a challenge to research that still reverberates throughout the field. At the beginning, postulation of the more primitive nature of the *Gospel of Thomas,* for example, was seen as something of an American perspective. In the meantime, however, this revolutionary perspective regarding early Christian noncanonical writings has spread across the scholarly world. The once academic demand to study the New Testament writings in the context of the other early Christian writings has become a reality in ever-increasing academic circles. College courses and books are tending to treat the New Testament and early Christian literature as a single subject. Students are discovering that their studies stand in continuity with the efforts of the Enlightenment to collect and evaluate all the documents of primitive Christianity.

The texts that New Testament scholars have begun to reconsider include not only those found near Nag Hammadi in Egypt and the fragments from Oxyrhynchos but also generally the writings classified as Christian apocrypha. A renewed search has ensued for manuscripts of these Christian apocrypha both in the West and in the East, especially among the neglected languages and traditions of the Christian orient. Simply on the basis of the number of languages and cultures involved, collaborative work among specialists from the various areas is required. Innumerable windows have been opened onto the vast sea of early Christian imagination. These fascinating vistas have indeed raised new questions about the ancient Christian tradition, also with respect to how it has been preserved in the canon.

This volume presents aspects of one of these new vistas on early Christianity, the traditions associated with the name Mary. New texts and known texts seen from the new perspective are raising new and old questions. Through the combination of these texts, an intriguing new type of Mary seems to have stepped forth. The *Gospel of Philip* from Nag Hammadi supplied the image of a Mary whom Jesus often kissed (*Gos. Phil.* 63.35–36), which quickly became indelible. This Mary is often given special revelations and stands in conflict with known male leaders in early Christianity, such as the twelve apostles. Modern feminist critique of ancient Christianity has consequently shown a particular interest in this Mary. At stake, in part, is the larger question of female leadership in Christianity, then and now. A theory has developed that this gnostic Mary, often called Mariamme, is none other than Mary Magdalene and that there was a "liberated" tradition under the auspices of Mary Magdalene from the earliest period onwards. A mounting volume of secondary literature has sprung up—so much, in fact, that one might speak of a new field of research into Mary(s). This literature, some of which is documented in the notes in this volume, is leading to the evolution of a new set of questions, such as: Why is the name "Mary" spelled differently in the texts, sometimes even within the same text? What happens to this name in the various relevant ancient languages? Are different Marys involved, with the forms of the name (Maria, Mariam, Mariamme, etc.) attached to different traditions? If so, have these traditions been intermingled so that research is justified to postulate a "generic Mary" for the ancient Christian tradition? It is among this second-generation set of questions that the essays in this volume belong. One finds here both answers suggested for known questions as well as attempts to reframe the entire discussion through new sorts of questions.

Such questions of the precise identity of Mary in early Christian texts dominate the first group of contributions to this volume. In the opening essay, Stephen Shoemaker immediately throws a wrench into the works of the developing theory regarding Mary Magdalene. Shoemaker argues that in many cases the Mary who has been assumed to be Mary Magdalene could actually be Mary the mother of Jesus. He first reviews, examines, and rejects the consensus that the form of the name Mary is a reliable indicator of the identity of the intended person. Next, he reexamines the profile of the mother of Jesus in early Christianity. Shoemaker convincingly brings to bear the fact that there has been an intermingling of traditions regarding the various Marys in ancient Christian tradition. He draws special attention to the text of Tatian's Gospel harmony, the *Diatessaron,* whose effect on Eastern Christian traditions is often overlooked. For Shoemaker, the "gnostic Mary" is a curious composite figure who requires careful handling. In any event, Shoemaker's study reflects the workshop of someone who is attempting to survey the enormous spectrum of Christian traditions, Eastern and Western.

A leading figure in the development of the consensus questioned by Shoemaker, Antti Marjanen, next reviews the history of research from his perspective. Marjanen responds to Shoemaker point by point. He makes some concessions but holds his ground in other places. Ultimately, Marjanen rejects Shoemaker's use of the Dormition apocrypha for the interpretation of the so-called gnostic writings. For Marjanen, the Mary in these last writings should still be identified with Mary Magdalene.

Ann Brock picks up at precisely this point to examine the evidence in one particular case, the long Coptic text known as *Pistis Sophia.* Here one sees the ins and outs of the exegetical arguments: the text is broken down into its component parts, and epithets of the Marys are closely analyzed. Brock concludes that in this text "the blessed one" and "the pure spiritual one" unambiguously designate Mary Magdalene and give her exceptional prominence: the Magdalene is the main Mary in *Pistis Sophia.* Incidentally, Brock's doctoral dissertation, which is repeatedly cited in the essays, will soon be more broadly available in the form of a monograph from Harvard University Press under the title *Mary Magdalene, the First Apostle: The Struggle for Authority.*

Karen King similarly pulls another critical ancient text under the magnifying glass, the *Gospel of Mary.* King raises the questions of whether, to what degree, and why it is significant that a Mary is a central figure of this text. These new questions about "figuration" (the type of individual represented in Mary as well as in other early Christian characters) simultaneously fit this volume into its larger context. King's essay treats the reader to a major participant's summations of the voluminous recent discussion of apostolic authority and gender imagery in gnostic texts as well as feminist employment of such texts in the broader analysis of early Christianity. As the title of her essay indicates, King is tugging at the way the entire question about Mary is posed.

Finally, François Bovon turns to Mary in the newly recovered *Acts of Philip.* He first engages in the surprisingly complex and continuing exploration of the name "Mary": Why is the name spelled in different ways (Maria,

Mariam, Mariamme, etc.), in which cultural circles was this name used, and
so forth? Then he systematically reviews the evidence on Mary in the *Acts of
Philip,* which he was instrumental in reestablishing through the recovery and
edition of a Greek manuscript that contained a large otherwise unpreserved
section. Bovon finds in this text a liberated tradition of women's ministry
associated with Mary Magdalene under the name Mariamne.

The last two essays, by Jonathan Knight and George Zervos, take the
reader back into the earliest traditions regarding Mary the mother of Jesus.
Knight urges that the *Ascension of Isaiah* contains traditions on Mary that
come from the reservoir also employed in the Gospel of Matthew. The
potential of this thesis for the exegesis of Matthew is profound and is still
being explored by scholarship. Knight thus opens an exciting door into
precanonical traditions about Mary the mother of Jesus.

George Zervos supports Knight's thesis but makes the case that this
new critical perspective on the *Ascension of Isaiah* should also be extended
to some traditions in the *Protevangelium of James.* Zervos focuses on elements that the two texts have in common, in distinction to the canonical
gospels. That these elements have been so little studied in past research
reveals again how the investigations in this volume stand on the cutting
edge, and the growing edge, of contemporary historical-critical scholarship.

These studies not only document where scholarship has come but
also are indicative of where it must go. The reader will find that collected
together, the essays refract each other and so better disclose the distinctive contribution of each one. A select bibliography was graciously
provided by Ann Graham Brock. For yet further assistance, indexes were
assembled by Jaimie Chester, with the help of R. Sterling Spector and
Michelle Foley, three students of Religious Studies in Long Beach. Bob
Buller prepared the book for production with great skill.

The papers in this volume have all been revised by the contributors
since their oral presentation in November 2000. At points, however, the
origin of the essays in the session "There's Something about Mary(s)" is still
clearly reflected. These remnants may serve as a reminder of the sociological context of all human research—in this case, the Society of Biblical
Literature on the brink of a new millennium.

A Case of Mistaken Identity?
Naming the Gnostic Mary[1]

Stephen J. Shoemaker
University of Oregon

One day, sometime after the Savior's ascension, a Great Angel, the Great Cherub of Light, appears to Mary and hands her a book of "mysteries," containing all the secrets of creation.[2] After telling Mary to deliver these secrets to the apostles, the Great Angel instructs her to ascend the Mount of Olives, where he will further reveal the mysteries of the universe to her. When she reaches the summit, the Great Angel discloses that he is in fact the Savior himself, the heavenly being that became incarnate in Jesus of Nazareth to bring humanity the message of salvation. Then the Great Angel begins a lengthy revelation discourse in which he entrusts Mary with several important "mysteries," instructing her to deliver them to the apostles in secret. Among these mysteries is a secret prayer, which the Savior instructs Mary must be spoken in order to ascend from this world past its demiurge, who is described as "a beast with the body of a lion and the tail of a snake." The Great Angel briefly explains the need for such a prayer by recounting Adam's creation by the "Ruler," and the need for his descendants to return to their true home with God in the fullness.

---

[1] Parts of this article were presented in earlier versions at the AAR Southeast Regional Meeting, Knoxville, March 1998; the North American Patristics Society Annual Meeting, Chicago, May 1998; and the SBL Annual Meeting, Nashville, November 2000. I would like to thank the following individuals for their contributions to this article: Melissa M. Aubin, Jorunn Jacobson Buckley, Elizabeth A. Clark, Deirdre Good, Philip Sellew, and Karen King, who kindly forwarded her comments on an earlier version of this argument that appeared in my dissertation.

[2] The following summary is from the *Liber Requiei,* an early account of Mary's departure from this world, edited by Victor Arras, *De transitu Mariae apocrypha aethiopice* (2 vols.; CSCO 343, 352, CSCO.Ae 67, 69; Leuven: Secrétariat du Corpus SCO, 1973), esp. sections 1–25. A critical, English translation of this narrative will appear in Stephen J. Shoemaker, *The Ancient Traditions of the Virgin Mary's Dormition and Assumption* (Oxford Early Christian Studies; Oxford: Clarendon, forthcoming).

The Savior again reminds Mary that she must teach this prayer to the apostles, which she later does, so that they "will tell the mystery to those who
believe, and the one to whom it is given will hear."

This portrait of Mary is not an altogether unfamiliar one: it resonates
nicely with the other images of Mary found elsewhere in early Christian
apocrypha, yet with one important exception. While scholarship has settled
in rather comfortably with the notion that the apocryphal Mary to whom the
Savior communicates the hidden mysteries of the cosmos is to be identified
with the Magdalene, the Mary represented in the ancient apocrypha that I
have just summarized is without any possible question Mary of Nazareth.
This episode is the opening sequence from the earliest extant narratives of
the end of Mary of Nazareth's earthly life, namely, the ancient Dormition
and Assumption apocrypha. Although there are over seventy different narratives of these events dating before the tenth century, between twenty and
twenty-five of these narratives, scattered among nine ancient languages, are
of particular importance for understanding the earliest history of these traditions. While many of these narratives include nothing like the Great
Angel's revelation to Mary, this episode is characteristic of the "Palm of the
Tree of Life" traditions, a group of related narratives that forms both the
largest textual family and the first to be attested.[3]

The earliest extant Dormition narrative, from which the above summary
is drawn, first appears in several Syriac fragments that were copied near
the end of the fifth century.[4] Other fragments survive in the tenth-century
Georgian homiliary tradition and some Coptic papyri from the seventh
century, but the narrative is known in its entirety only in the Ethiopic, as
is the case with other somewhat curious apocrypha, such as *Enoch* and
Jubilees.[5] Nevertheless, comparison with various ancient witnesses confirms

---

[3] For more on these narratives of the end of Mary's life, see my forthcoming
study: Shoemaker, *Dormition and Assumption*. In the interim, the best study published to date is Michel van Esbroeck, "Les textes littéraires sur l'assomption avant
le Xe siècle," in François Bovon et al., *Les actes apocryphes des apôtres* (Geneva:
Labor et Fides, 1981), 265–85.

[4] William Wright, *Contributions to the Apocryphal Literature* (London: Williams
& Norgate, 1865), ܡܗ–ܡܓ (Syriac) and 42–51 (English); for date, see pp. 6, 10–11.
Note also that Wright has elsewhere dated the earliest of these fragments to the
beginning of the sixth century: idem, *Catalogue of the Syriac Manuscripts of the
British Museum Acquired since the Year 1838* (3 vols.; London: Gilbert & Riving-
ton, 1870–72), 1:369.

[5] Georgian fragments: Michel van Esbroeck, "Apocryphes géorgiens de la Dormition," *AnBoll* 92 (1973): 55–75; these have also been edited in Tamila Mgaloblishvili,
კლარჯული მრავალთავი (*K'larjuli mravaltavi* [*The Homiliary of K'larjeti*]) (Tbil-
isi: "Metsnieba," 1991), 420–25. Coptic fragments: Eugène Revillout, *Évangile des*

the antiquity of this Ethiopic version, including especially two complete, but "edited," Greek narratives from the sixth and seventh centuries, as well as the entire Western narrative tradition, both in Latin and Irish. While we may only be certain of the narrative's existence by the late fifth century, as witnessed by the Syriac fragments, it is nevertheless evident that the Syriac version has been translated from an earlier Greek narrative, suggesting that the narrative reaches back at least to the early fifth century, if not even earlier. An earlier date is in fact suggested, but by no means secured, by the theologically peculiar ambiance of the narrative, including its angel Christology and the presence of certain classically "gnostic" themes, all of which would seem to indicate an existence as early as the second or third century, as many students of the Dormition apocrypha have observed.[6]

As such, these narratives present a rather interesting problem, one with which I have had to wrestle a great deal: What exactly is the relationship of one "gnostic" Mary to the other? That is, what connections might exist between the representation of Mary of Nazareth in the earliest Dormition apocrypha and the "other" Mary of the early Christian apocrypha. Oddly enough, this second woman's identity is only rarely specified in texts where she appears: in all but two instances, those being the *Gospel of Philip* and the *Pistis Sophia,* this woman is known only by the name "Mary," without any further clarification.[7] That is, the narratives do not specify that this woman is Mary the Magdalene, an equation that is generally assumed on the basis of other criteria. One might hope, as some have, that the problem could be resolved by appealing to the *Gospel of Philip* and the *Pistis Sophia,* where the Magdalene is in fact specifically identified. But this unfortunately does not settle the matter: in both the *Gospel of Philip* and the *Pistis Sophia* Mary of Nazareth is identified as an important figure in addition to Mary of Magdala. In regards to the *Gospel of Philip,* for instance, various scholars, including Jorunn Jacobson Buckley, Robert Murray, and Antti Marjanen, have come to the

---

douze apôtres (PO 2/2; Paris: Librairie de Paris/Firmin-Didot et Cie, 1907), 174–83. Other Coptic fragments have been published by Philip Sellew, "An Early Coptic Witness to the *Dormitio Mariae* at Yale: P. CtYBR inv. 1788 Revisited," *BASP* 37 (2000): 37–69. A preliminary edition was made by Leslie S. B. MacCoull, "More Coptic Papyri from the Beinecke Collection," *APF* 35 (1989): 25–35, with plate 4. Professor Sellew's edition offers a number of improved readings, and I thank him for sharing his work with me before its publication.

[6] These points are demonstrated in my forthcoming book, Shoemaker, *Dormition and Assumption.*

[7] On this and other points related to the present article, see my article also on this topic: Stephen J. Shoemaker, "Rethinking the 'Gnostic Mary': Mary of Nazareth and Mary of Magdala in Early Christian Tradition," *JECS* 9 (2001): 555–95.

recognition that "Mary" in this gospel is best understood as not being a single figure, but rather as a conflation of several different historical women.[8] This Mary, Philip tells us, is the Savior's mother, sister, and companion: as Marjanen writes of the *Gospel of Philip,* "The triple function of Mary shows that no historical person is meant."[9] Rather, the Mary of Philip is sometimes Mary of Magdala, sometimes Mary of Nazareth, but also a conflation of both. Scholars have suggested as much about Mary in other texts as well, including Marvin Meyer, who notes regarding Mary in the *Gospel of Thomas* that "a 'universal Mary' is in mind, and that specific historical Marys are no longer clearly distinguished,"[10] and Deirdre Good, who has recently suggested that the Mary of *Pistis Sophia* has a "composite identity," although she oddly fails to specify Mary of Nazareth as forming part of this composite.[11]

In regards to the *Pistis Sophia,* I strongly agree with Good's recognition of Mary's "composite identity" in this text, but with the important clarification that this composite draws predominately on Mary of Nazareth and Mary of Magdala, rather than Mary of Bethany and the "other women in the Gospels," as Good suggests. In this way the *Pistis Sophia* too fails to resolve this question of Mary's identity. Yet oddly enough, the *Pistis Sophia* in many ways represents the crux of the matter, for it would seem that this text more than any other set the course for the previous century's interpretation of this figure, largely, no doubt, because it was the first to be discovered. One of this text's earliest editors and translators, Carl Schmidt, seems to have given birth to the notion that the Mary who figures so prominently in the *Pistis Sophia* is to be identified with the Magdalene, and not Mary of Nazareth. The most prominent of the Savior's interlocutors in the *Pistis Sophia* is alternatively named either Maria or

---

[8] Antti Marjanen, *The Woman Jesus Loved: Mary Magdalene in the Nag Hammadi Library and Related Documents* (Nag Hammadi and Manichaean Studies 40; Leiden: Brill, 1996), 160–61; Robert Murray, *Symbols of Church and Kingdom: A Study in Early Syriac Tradition* (London: Cambridge University Press, 1975), 333; Jorunn Jacobson Buckley, "'The Holy Spirit' Is a Double Name," in *Female Fault and Fulfilment in Gnosticism* (Chapel Hill: University of North Carolina Press, 1986), 105.

[9] Marjanen, *The Woman Jesus Loved,* 160–61.

[10] Marvin W. Meyer, "Making Mary Male: The Categories 'Male' and 'Female' in the Gospel of Thomas," *NTS* 31 (1985): 562. The passage in question is *Gos. Thom.* 114 (Bentley Layton, ed., *Gospel according to Thomas, Gospel according to Philip, Hypostasis of the Archons, and Indices* [vol. 1 of *Nag Hammadi Codex II,2–7 together with XIII,2*, Brit. Lib. Or. 4926[1], and P. Oxy. 1, 654, 655;* NHS 20; Leiden: Brill, 1989], 92–93), where Jesus speaks of "making Mary male."

[11] Deirdre Good, "Pistis Sophia," in *Searching the Scriptures* (ed. E. Schüssler Fiorenza; 2 vols.; New York: Crossroad, 1993–94), 2:696, 703–4.

Mariam,[12] names that could refer potentially to either Mary of Nazareth or Mary Magdalene, both of whom are occasionally specified as participants in the dialogue.[13] But these moments of clarity are rare, and with only these few exceptions the Mary who speaks with the risen Christ is not otherwise identified. Despite Ernest Renan's early suggestion that this Mary is Mary of Nazareth, scholars have persistently followed the lead of Schmidt, who explicitly rejected Renan's interpretation and identified this figure with the Magdalene.[14] Students of early Christianity have by now grown quite comfortable with the notion that this figure represents Mary of Magdala and not Mary of Nazareth. So pervasive has this identification become that one might hardly think to question it. In fact, it is somewhat difficult to challenge this interpretation, since it is often assumed or asserted rather than explained,[15] making it sometimes unclear exactly what one is arguing against.[16]

1. Maria, Mariam, and Mariamme: What's in a Name?

The gnostic Mary was first restored to history by the discovery of the *Pistis Sophia* in 1773,[17] and one of this text's earliest editors and translators, Carl Schmidt, seems to have given birth to the notion that the Mary who figures so prominently in this text is to be identified with the Magdalene, and not Mary of Nazareth. Schmidt's early decisions regarding Mary in the *Pistis Sophia* have subsequently extended their influence to

---

[12] There is also a single usage of ΜΑΡΙϨΑΜΜΗ: *Pistis Sophia* 133 (Carl Schmidt, ed., *Pistis Sophia* [trans. V. MacDermot; NHS 9; Leiden: Brill, 1978], 346).

[13] Mary the mother of Jesus: Schmidt, *Pistis Sophia,* 13, 116, 117, 120, 123, 124, 125. Mary the Magdalene: ibid., 185, 189, 199, 201, 203, 218, 233, 237, 244, 319, 338.

[14] Carl Schmidt, *Gnostiche Schriften in koptischer Sprache aus dem Codex Brucianus* (TU 8/1; Leipzig: Hinrichs, 1892), 453–54, esp. n. 1, and 597, esp. n. 2.

[15] See J. Kevin Coyle, "Mary Magdalene in Manichaeism?" *Mus* 104 (1991): 41–42, where he notes that despite this figure's significant ambiguities, "undaunted, virtually all commentators on the Gnostic writings identify their «Mary» (or one of them) as the Magdalene, although this identification is explicit only in [*Gos. Phil.*] and *Pistis Sophia*"; as we will see, however, the identity of "Mary" even in these texts is more complex than Coyle here suggests.

[16] But see Marjanen, *The Woman Jesus Loved*. Nevertheless, this work too seems to assume more than it argues on this matter, and, as will be seen below, it relies too heavily on a supposed distinction between the use of the names "Maria" and "Mariam," which I will show to be falsely made.

[17] Carl Schmidt, *Koptisch-gnostische Schriften* (vol. 1; 4th ed.; GCS 45; Berlin: Akademie-Verlag, 1981), xvi.

determine the understanding of the many Coptic "gnostic" texts that have since been discovered. These include the *Gospel of Mary,* whose manuscript Schmidt acquired for the Berlin Museum in 1896, and the various Nag Hammadi texts that mention a woman named Mary.

From Schmidt's early commentaries, the firm notion has developed that the forms of the name Mariam and Mariamme, as opposed to Maria, reliably indicate the Magdalene's presence, with some scholars even going so far as to assert that Mary of Nazareth is always specifically identified in early Christian literature, making any unspecified Mary a reference to Mary of Magdala.[18] In discussions of the gnostic Mary's identity, one finds this sort of argumentation everywhere: it is always a primary argument, and with very few exceptions[19] it is usually the only evidence of this woman's identity that is offered.[20] Most recently it has found expression in Antti

---

[18] Although it is somewhat difficult to trace the development of this hermeneutic principle, it appears to have its origin in Schmidt's early decisions concerning the different Marys of the *Pistis Sophia.* Firstly, Schmidt suggests that the character known simply as Mary in the *Pistis Sophia* is always to be identified as Mary of Magdala, whether or not her identity as the Magdalene is specified, while the mother of Jesus is present in the dialogue only when Mary of Nazareth is explicitly indicated. Schmidt's second contribution was to identify this Mary with a woman (or perhaps women?) named Mariamme, whom Origen (actually, Celsus) and Hippolytus associated with early Christian heterodoxy. Presumably, it was this equation that birthed the notion that the names Mariamme and, by association (?), Mariam were infallible indicators of the Magdalene's presence in a text. See especially Schmidt, *Koptisch-gnostische Schriften,* 452–54, 563–64.

[19] This is true especially of Karen L. King, "The Gospel of Mary Magdalene," in *Searching the Scriptures,* 2:618–20; and seemingly also of Michel Tardieu, *Écrits gnostiques: Codex de Berlin* (Sources gnostiques et manichéenes 1; Paris: Cerf, 1984), who for the most part simply assumes this, but at one point he does suggest that her identity is related to her status as the first witness to the resurrection (225).

[20] Schmidt's conclusions are often cited in this context (see n. 14 above), and while he is not as clear on the Mariam/Mariamme/Maria distinction, he does seemingly generate the notion that an otherwise unidentified Mary is to be equated with the Magdalene. See also Silke Petersen, *"Zerstört die Werke der Weiblichkeit!" Maria Magdalena, Salome und andere Jüngerinnen Jesu in christlich-gnostischen Schriften* (Nag Hammadi and Manichaean Studies 48; Leiden: Brill, 1999), 94; Anne Pasquier, *L'Évangile selon Marie* (BCNH.T 10; Québec: Les presses de l'Université Laval, 1983), 23 n. 75; Coyle, "Mary Magdalene in Manichaeism?"; Susan Haskins, *Mary Magdalene: Myth and Metaphor* (New York: Harcourt Brace, 1993), 37; Richard Atwood, Mary *Magdalene in the New Testament Gospels and Early Tradition* (Bern: Lang, 1993), 186–96, largely assumes the identity of this figure with the Magdalene, but the repeated emphasis on the form of the name seems to suggest that Atwood has this principle in mind; Esther de Boer, *Mary Magdalene: Beyond the Myth*

Marjanen's study, *The Woman Jesus Loved: Mary Magdalene in the Nag Hammadi Library and Related Documents.*[21] One of this work's guiding principles is that "in all those Coptic texts where Mary is explicitly defined as the (virgin) mother of Jesus the name is without exception spelled ⲘⲀⲢⲒⲀ while the form of the name used of Mary Magdalene is almost always ⲘⲀⲢⲒ(ϩ)ⲀⲘ(ⲘⲎ)."[22]

Marjanen continues with the additional assertion that Christian Greek prefers the use of Μαρία to Μαριάμ in reference to the Virgin,[23] and in his study, he relies heavily on a supposedly firm distinction in the usage of these different nominal variants to identify the gnostic Mary with the Magdalene.[24] In doing so, Marjanen follows over a century worth of scholarly consensus on these points. Unfortunately, however, despite this strong

---

(Harrisburg, Pa.: Trinity Press International, 1997), 81; Renate Schmid, *Maria Magdalena in gnostischen Schriften* (Munich: Arbeitsgemeinschaft für Religions- und Weltanschauungsfragen, 1990), 93 n. 9 and 101 n. 29, addresses the question of Mary's identity in light of the variant names, further explaining, "Daß dabei jedoch immer M[aria] M[agdalena] gemeint ist zeigt die Tatsache, daß es keine Stelle gibt, an der die Charakterisierung der Frau eher auf die Mutter als auf M[aria] M[agdalena] zutreffen würde, diese aber nicht als solche bezeichnet wird. Die Mutter Maria ist immer als solche genau bestimmt"; François Bovon, "Le privilège pascal de Marie-Madeleine," *NTS* 30 (1984): 50–62, repeatedly emphasizes the significance of the form of the name, assuming its importance, without ever really explaining why.

[21] Marjanen, *The Woman Jesus Loved.*

[22] Ibid., 63–64. Marjanen's constant references back to this passage and its related footnotes throughout his work illustrate just how significant this distinction is for his identification of this woman with the Magdalene. See the examples collected in n. 24 below.

[23] Ibid., 63–64 n. 33, where he gives a few references to the antiheretical works of Irenaeus, Hippolytus, and Epiphanius, noting only one major exception to his claim, the use of Μαριάμμη in the *Protevangelium of James.*

[24] This argument is most prominently featured in Marjanen's discussion of *Sophia of Jesus Christ,* where he explains the importance of the different variants (ibid., 62–63), a passage that is often cross-referenced in discussion of subsequent texts. Other texts for which this is the primary or only argument given for Mary's identity with the Magdalene include: *Gospel of Thomas* (p. 39); *Gospel of Mary* (pp. 94–95); (*First*) *Apocalypse of James* (p. 131); *Pistis Sophia* (pp. 173–74 and 184 n. 43); *The Manichean Psalm Book* (pp. 206–7; see especially n. 11 here, where the importance of name spelling is emphasized). Although Marjanen sometimes gives the appearance of relying on other criteria, such as conflict with the apostles (*Gospel of Thomas*), the "Philip group" (*Sophia of Jesus Christ*), etc., many of these will be seen to rest ultimately on decisions about Mary's identity in other texts, where the decision is based primarily on this criterion.

consensus, none of these presuppositions holds true, and in fact, they are demonstrably false: the form of the name Mary alone does not reliably distinguish between these two women and so in no way can guarantee their distinction in early Christian literature.

Turning first to Greek Christian literature, one need not pass beyond the New Testament, where one discovers that Μαριάμ is the predominant biblical name for the mother of Jesus, while it is the Magdalene who is generally known as Μαρία.[25] Likewise, the writings of the early church fathers follow suit, using the name Mariam almost exclusively in reference to the Virgin:[26] Origen, Eusebius, Gregory of Nyssa, Athanasius, Epiphanius, John Chrysostom, Didymus the Blind, Theodoret, John Malalas, and Romanos the Melodist, among others, all frequently refer to the Virgin as Μαριάμ, while Mary Magdalene is almost always known as Μαρία.[27] So too the early Christian apocrypha preserved in Greek often use the name Μαριάμ for Mary of Nazareth, including, for instance, certain of the apocryphal acts,[28] as well as the second-century *Protevangelium of James*[29] and the third-century *Gospel (Questions) of Bartholomew,*[30] both

---

[25] See Émile de Strycker, *La forme la plus ancienne du Protévangile de Jacques* (SHG 33; Brussels: Société des Bollandistes, 1961), 316. In the twenty-sixth edition of the Nestle-Aland *Novum Testamentum Graece,* the Virgin is called Μαριάμ in Matt 1:20; 13:55; Luke 1:27, 30, 34, 38, 39, 46, 56; 2:5, 16, 19, 34; Acts 1:14, and she is known as Μαρία in Matt 1:16, 18; 2:11; Mark 6:3; Luke 1:41. The Magdalene, on the other hand, generally passes as Μαρία (this is also Atwood's conclusion [*Mary Magdalene,* 133]), as in Matt 27:56; Mark 15:40, 47; 16:1, 9; Luke 8:2; 24:10; John 19:25; 20:1, 11, and is only known as Μαριάμ in Matt 27:61; 28:1; John 20:16, 18. Μαριάμ is also used for Martha's sister Mary: Luke 10:39, 42; John 11:2, 19, 20, 28, 31, 32, 45; 12:3. Nevertheless, the critical apparatus of this edition reveals that in many of these instances there is a substantial manuscript tradition supporting the use of the other name.

[26] And of course also for the sister of Moses.

[27] Hundreds of such references were obtained for these and other authors by searching the first through sixth century C.E. materials on the *Thesaurus Linguae Grecae* CD ROM D for Μαριάμ and Μαγδαληνή.

[28] As noted by Coyle, "Mary Magdalene in Manichaeism?" 41, although his references are to the somewhat later (fifth/sixth century) *Acts of Andrew and Matthias* and *Acts of Bartholomew.*

[29] See de Strycker, *La forme la plus ancienne,* 315–16, as well as the discussion below.

[30] *Gos. Bart.* 2.2; 2.5; 2.11; 2.22; 4.10 (A. Vassiliev, ed., *Anecdota Graeco-Byzantina,* pt. 1 [Moscow: Universitas Caesareae, 1893], 11, 12, 14; A. Wilmart and E. Tisserant, "Fragments grecs et latins de l'Évangile de Barthélemy," *RB* 10 [1913]: 321–23, 325, 329).

of which use the names Maria and Mariam interchangeably in reference to Mary of Nazareth.

The latter of these texts, the *Gospel (Questions) of Bartholomew,* is of particular importance, since its portrait of Mary of Nazareth compares favorably with both the gnostic apocrypha and certain other late ancient depictions of the Virgin Mary as one who teaches cosmic mysteries to the apostles. Probably composed in third-century Egypt, this text, although perhaps not "properly gnostic," betrays certain gnostic leanings.[31] Most importantly, however, among its main characters stands a certain Mary, known both as Μαρία and Μαριάμ, whom the context unambiguously identifies as Mary of Nazareth.[32] This narrative presents the Virgin Mary as an authority on the cosmic mysteries, whose teaching the apostles highly esteem and repeatedly seek. When at their bidding she begins to reveal certain mysteries, her son interrupts and commands her to stop.[33] This composite invites comparison with the character known as Maria or Mariam in the Coptic gnostic texts, who also instructs the apostles concerning the gnostic mysteries, in which she is similarly gifted.

Significantly less comparative evidence exists for the name Mariamme. Despite its occasional presence in the Coptic apocrypha, it is rather uncommon in Christian Greek, where to my knowledge it occurs in only seven texts from before the seventh century.[34] In three of these, the usage

---

[31] Wilhelm Schneemelcher, ed., *New Testament Apocrypha* (trans. R. McL. Wilson; 2 vols.; rev. ed.; Cambridge: Clarke; Louisville: Westminster John Knox, 1991–92), 1:538–40.

[32] "Let us ask Mary [Μαριάμ], her who is highly favored, how she conceived the incomprehensible or how she carried him who cannot be carried or how she bore so much greatness" (*Gos. Bart.* 2.2; Vassiliev, *Anecdota Graeco-Byzantina,* 11; Wilmart and Tisserant, "Fragments grecs et latins," 321; translation from Schneemelcher, *New Testament Apocrypha,* 1:543).

[33] *Gos. Bart.* 2.1–22 (Vassiliev, *Anecdota Graeco-Byzantina,* 11–14; Wilmart and Tisserant, "Fragments grecs et latins," 321–25). See also *Gos. Bart.* 4.1–6 (Vassiliev, *Anecdota Graeco-Byzantina,* 14–15; Wilmart and Tisserant, "Fragments grecs et latins," 327–28).

[34] This was verified by searching the *Thesaurus Linguae Grecae* CD ROM D for Μαριάμμη. I exclude here the occurrence of Mariamme in the *Gospel of Mary,* since this ambiguous usage is among the matters in question. This instance is, however, discussed in some detail below. The name Mariamme also appears in two (or perhaps three) Syrian inscriptions, noted in Heinz Wuthnow, *Die semitischen Menschennamen in griechischen Inschriften und Papyri des vorderen Orients* (Studien zur Epigraphik und Papyruskunde 1/4; Leipzig: Dieterich'sche Verlagsbuchhandlung, 1930), 73, although the referents are otherwise unknown. See also de Strycker, *La forme la plus ancienne,* 316. Josephus of course frequently uses this name for Herod's wife.

depends on Josephus and therefore has neither the Virgin nor the Magdalene in mind, referring instead to Herod's wife.[35] But the pagan
philosopher Celsus mentions a Christian group named after a certain Mariamme, who is otherwise unidentified.[36] Perhaps this group bears some
relation to the "Nassenes" of Hippolytus's *Refutatio,* whose teachings were
supposedly passed down from James the brother of the Lord through a
woman named Mariamne.[37] The name Mariamme also occurs in the *Acts
of Philip,* probably composed during the fourth or fifth century, where this
is the name of Philip's sister.[38] Soon after this Mariamne appears, the Savior identifies her as "blessed among women," a Lukan epithet that seems
to identify her with Mary of Nazareth, as does reference to Mariamne's having "escaped the poverty of Eve, so as to enrich herself." The later point
resonates especially with Mary's identity in late antiquity as the "new Eve,"
whose actions remove the curse of the "old" Eve. This Mariamne's identity
is obviously much more complex than this might suggest, however, since
she is also Philip's sister, and there also seems to be an attempt to connect
her with the Mary of "Mary and Martha" fame.

In each of these instances, there is no clear indication that the
Mariamme in question is either Mary of Nazareth or the Magdalene, an
identification made only, to my knowledge, in the third-century Bodmer

---

[35] Didymus the Blind, *Comm. Eccl.* 174.15–24 (Johannes Kramer et al., eds.,
Didymos der Blinde: Kommentar zum Ecclesiastes [6 vols.; PTA 9, 13, 16, 22, 24, 25;
Bonn: Habelt, 1969–79], 3:70–71); Eusebius, *Dem. ev.* 8.2.93 (Ivar Heikel, ed., *Die
Demonstratio evangelica* [vol. 6 of *Eusebius Werke;* GCS 23; Leipzig: Hinrichs,
1913], 384); idem, *Ecl. proph.* 3.46 (PG 22:1135).

[36] Origen, *Cels.* 5.62 (Marcel Borret, ed., *Origène: Contre Celse* [5 vols.; SC 132,
136, 147, 150, 227; Paris: Cerf, 1967–76], 2:168–69).

[37] Hippolytus, *Haer.* 5.7.1, 10.9.3 (Miroslav Marcovich, ed., *Hippolytus: Refutatio
omnium haeresium* [PTS 25; Berlin: de Gruyter, 1986], 142, 384).

[38] François Bovon, Bertrand Bouvier, and Frédéric Amsler, *Acta Philippi* (2 vols.;
CCSA 11–12; Turnhout: Brepols, 1999), esp. 1:240–47. These scholars have generally assumed that this woman should be connected with the gnostic Mary, with
which I agree. On this basis, it is further assumed (without sufficient explanation)
that this Mariamne is Mary of Magdala, with which I do not agree. The only arguments given for identifying the Mary of the *Acts of Philip* with the Magdalene are
several references to the various gnostic Mary traditions (see Bovon, Bouvier, and
Amsler, *Acta Philippi,* 2:312–17; and Bovon, "Le privilège pascal," esp. 57–58). Nevertheless, I have elsewhere demonstrated that each of these gnostic Mary texts are
themselves problematic with regard to the identification of their Mary with either
the Magdalene or the Nazarene (see Shoemaker, "Rethinking the 'Gnostic Mary'").
Therefore, one can no longer lean on these as if they can fix the identity of any
Mary who appears in an apocryphal text.

papyrus of the *Protevangelium of James*,[39] where Mary of Nazareth is several times named Mariamme.[40] There is no similar instance in Greek where the name Mariamme is used specifically for the Magdalene, and although later manuscripts of the *Protevangelium* have not preserved this early variant, these versions generally prefer the name Mariam instead of Maria in reference to Mary of Nazareth,[41] confirming Christian Greek's preference for calling the Mary of Nazareth, rather than the Magdalene, by the name Mariam. The weight of the Greek evidence then strongly favors the identification of an otherwise unspecified Mariam or Mariamme not with the Magdalene, but with Mary of Nazareth. The clear tendency of Christian Greek writers from the Gospels to the early apocrypha to the church fathers is to use the names Mariam and even Mariamme primarily in reference to Mary of Nazareth rather than to Mary of Magdala.

Nevertheless, since the majority of these gnostic Mary traditions have been preserved in Coptic, we must also consider the naming of the different Marys in the Coptic tradition. Although these Coptic apocrypha were almost certainly translated from Greek originals,[42] the usage of these names in Coptic is undoubtedly an important point of comparison. As one examines the Coptic literature of late antiquity, one finds, as in Greek, liberal usage of the name Mariam in reference to Mary of Nazareth. This is particularly true of perhaps the earliest and most influential of Coptic texts, the translations of the New Testament,[43] where the mother of Christ and

---

[39] For the date, see Michel Testuz, ed., *Nativité de Marie* (Papyrus Bodmer 5; Geneva: Bibliotheca Bodmeriana, 1958), 23–26.

[40] *Prot. Jas.* 16.3, 17.2, 17.3 (Testuz, *Nativité de Marie*, 98, 100, 102).

[41] De Strycker, *La forme la plus ancienne*, 315.

[42] Bentley Layton, *The Gnostic Scriptures* (Garden City, N.Y.: Doubleday, 1987), xxv–xxvii; James M. Robinson, ed., *The Nag Hammadi Library in English* (rev. ed.; San Francisco: Harper & Row, 1988), 2, 12.

[43] Both the Sahidic and Bohairic translations were made during the late antique period, the Sahidic probably in the third or the fourth century and the Bohairic probably in the fifth or sixth century: Bruce M. Metzger, *The Early Versions of the New Testament: Their Origin, Transmission, and Limitations* (Oxford: Clarendon, 1977), 125–32. Frederik Wisse, however, notes the existence of the "few early Bohairic fragments" mentioned in Metzger, *Early Versions of the New Testament*, 123–25, but considers these "idiosyncratic" and not "in an obvious relationship with the later Bohairic version." This later Bohairic version he dates to the ninth century. Wisse agrees, however, with the dating of the Sahidic version: Frederik Wisse, "The Coptic Versions of the New Testament," in *The Text of the New Testament in Contemporary Research: Essays on the* Status Quaestionis (ed. B. D. Ehrman and M. W. Holmes; Grand Rapids: Eerdmans, 1995), 134–36. But see Metzger, *Early Versions of the New Testament*, 126 and 131, where he summarizes the view of

the Magdalene are equally called both Mariam and Maria. Thus we might ask along with the Sahidic Gospel of Matthew: "Is not his mother she whom they are wont to call, Mariham?"[44] One could hardly ask for clearer or more authoritative evidence of this fact: these foundational texts of Coptic culture repeatedly identify the mother of Christ with the name Mariam.[45]

Moreover, this practice is by no means unique to the Coptic New Testament, but it is present in both the Coptic apocryphal and homiletic traditions. In the Coptic *Gospel of Bartholomew*,[46] for instance, an apocryphon from the fifth or sixth century, Mary of Nazareth's name is Mariam.[47] Likewise, in the various Coptic homilies attributed to Cyril of Jerusalem, Mary of Nazareth is known as Mariam. For instance, a pseudo-Cyrilline homily on the passion, probably from the early seventh century, explains that both Mary of Nazareth and Mary Magdalene shared the name Mariam, because the Magdalene was Anne's sister, and out of love for her sister, Anne chose to name her daughter Mariam.[48] Similarly, in pseudo-Cyril's

---

Rudolph Kasser that the beginnings of the Bohairic version were in the fourth and fifth century and that during the sixth century the Bohairic version reached its classic form. On the New Testament's primacy in Coptic literature and culture, see Roger S. Bagnall, *Egypt in Late Antiquity* (Princeton, N.J.: Princeton University Press, 1993), 238–40.

[44] ⲘⲎ ⲚⲦⲉϥⲘⲀⲀⲨ ⲀⲚ ⲦⲈ ϢⲀⲨⲘⲞⲨⲦⲈ ⲈⲢⲞⲤ ϪⲈ ⲘⲀⲢⲒⳍⲀⲘ: Matt 13:55 (George William Horner, *The Coptic Version of the New Testament in the Southern Dialect* [7 vols.; Oxford: Clarendon, 1911–24], 1:138–39).

[45] For the version of the New Testament linguistically nearest to the Coptic apocrypha in question, see Horner, *Coptic New Testament in the Southern Dialect,* where the Virgin is called Mariam at Matt 13:55; 27:56; Mark 6:3 (1:138, 340–42, 428–29); John 20:18 (3:316); and Acts 1:14 (6:10, and E. A. Wallis Budge, *Coptic Biblical Texts in the Dialect of Upper Egypt* [London: British Museum, 1912], 124). In Bohairic such usage is quite common. See George William Horner, *The Coptic Version of the New Testament in the Northern Dialect* (4 vols.; Oxford: Clarendon, 1898), passim; e.g., Luke 1:27–2:5 (2:8–21).

[46] N.B., this is an entirely different text from the Greek *Gospel (Questions) of Bartholomew* discussed above.

[47] E.g., E. A. Wallis Budge, *Coptic Apocrypha in the Dialect of Upper Egypt* (London: British Museum, 1913), 12, 31–32, 42; Pierre Lacau, *Fragments d'apocryphes coptes* (vol. 9 of *Mémoires publiés par les membres de l'institut français d'archéologie orientale du Caire;* Cairo: Imprimerie de l'institut français d'archéologie orientale, 1904), 51. For the date, see Schneemelcher, *New Testament Apocrypha,* 1:537; and J. K. Elliott, *The Apocryphal New Testament* (Oxford: Clarendon, 1993), 652.

[48] Ⲁ ⲦⲈⳌⳠⲰⲚⲈ ⲞⲨⲚ ⲘⲀⲄⲆⲀⲖⲒⲚⲎ ⲈⲦⲂⲈ ⲠⲈⳠⲚⲞ6 ⲘⲘⲈ ⲈⳌⲞⲨⲚ ⲈⲢⲞⳠ ⲀⳠⲘⲞⲨⲦⲈ ⲈⲢⲞⳠ ⲘⲠⲈⳠⲢⲀⲚ ⲘⲘⲒⲚ ⲘⲘⲞⳠ. ϪⲈ ⲘⲀⲢⲒⳍⲀⲘ˙ Ⲁ ⲠⲀⲒ ϢⲰⲠⲈ ⲚⲀⲒⲀⲫⲞⲢⲀ ⲘⲠⲢⲀⲚ ⳠⲚⲀⲨ, Pseudo-Cyril of Jerusalem, *Homily on the Passion I 5–6*

homily on the Dormition, probably composed in the late fifth or early sixth century, the Virgin Mary's name is "Maria, which is interpreted, Mariam," and because her native village was "Magdalia," she was also called Mary Magdalene.[49] So not only was the name Mariam used equally in Coptic for both the Virgin and the Magdalene, but in the minds of some, the two were actually thought to have been the same person. Although this same narrative later contradicts its own conflation,[50] it remains that not only were the names Maria and Mariam easily interchangeable, but so also at times were the characters themselves. The identities of the Virgin and the Magdalene were often merged in late antiquity, a fact that in itself should warn us against any easy assumption that ancient Coptic speakers differentiated between Maria, the Virgin, and Mariam, the Magdalene with the precision that modern scholarship has suggested.[51]

2. "Woman, Behold Thy Son"/"I Have Seen the Lord": Mary of Nazareth and Mary of Magdala in Early Christian Tradition

While ancient usage of the various forms of "Mary" has figured prominently in this history of this "Magdalenenfrage," several scholars have also sought to cement the gnostic Mary's identity with reference to the Magdalene's importance elsewhere in early Christian literature. With

---

(Antonella Campagnano, *Ps. Cirillo di Gerusalemme: Omelie copte sulla passione, sulla croce e sulla vergine* [TDSA 65; Milan: Cisalpiono-Goliardica, 1980], 28). See also later in the text where the risen Christ appears to his mother, who is called Mariam: ⲁⲩⲱ ⲙ̅ⲡⲛⲁⲩ ⲛ̅ϫⲡ̅ⲙⲏⲧⲉ ⲛ̅ⲧⲉⲩϣⲏ ⲛ̅ⲧⲕ̅ⲩⲣⲓⲁⲕⲏ ⲛ̅ⲧⲁϥⲟⲩⲟⲛϩϥ̅ ⲉⲙⲁⲣⲓϩⲁⲙ ⲧⲉϥ-ⲙⲁⲁⲩ, *Homily on the Passion I* 29 (ibid., 44). The date is discussed in ibid., 14.

[49] ⲙⲁⲣⲓⲁ, ⲧⲉⲧϣⲁⲩⲟⲩⲁϩⲙⲉⲥ ϫⲉ ⲙⲁⲣⲓϩⲁⲙ ... ⲁⲛⲟⲕ ⲧⲉ ⲙⲁⲣⲓⲁ ⲧⲙⲁⲕ-ⲇⲁⲗⲓⲛⲏ, ⲉⲧⲉ ⲡⲣⲁⲛ ⲙ̅ⲡⲁ†ⲙⲉ ⲡⲉ ⲙⲁⲕⲇⲁⲗⲓⲁ, Pseudo-Cyril of Jerusalem, *Homily on the Dormition* 10 (Campagnano, *Ps. Cirillo*, 158; and E. A. Wallis Budge, *Miscellaneous Coptic Texts in the Dialect of Upper Egypt* [London: British Museum, 1915], 52–53). For the date, see Simon C. Mimouni, *Dormition et assomption de Marie: Histoire des traditions anciennes* (ThH 98; Paris: Beauchesne, 1995), 193–94.

[50] Near the end of this narrative, the Virgin entrusts those virgins living with her to the care of Mary Magdalene, who is now clearly identified as a separate person: ⲁⲥⲁⲙⲁϩⲧⲉ ⲛ̅ⲧϭⲓϫ ⲛⲟⲩⲉⲓ ⲉⲃⲟⲗ ⲛ̅ϩⲏⲧⲟⲩ ⲉⲁⲥⲣ̅ ϩⲁⲗⲱ ⲉⲧⲉ ⲙⲁⲣⲓⲁ ⲧⲙⲁⲅ-ⲇⲁⲗⲓⲛⲏ ⲧⲉ, ⲧⲏ ⲛ̅ⲧⲁ ⲡⲉⲭ̅ⲥ̅ ⲛⲉϫ ⲡⲥⲁϣϥ̅ ⲛ̅ⲇⲁⲓⲙⲟⲛⲓⲟⲛ ⲉⲃⲟⲗ ⲛ̅ϩⲏⲧⲥ, Pseudo-Cyril of Jerusalem, *Homily on the Dormition* 46 (Campagnano, *Ps. Cirillo*, 186; and Budge, *Miscellaneous Coptic Texts*, 68–69).

[51] See, in addition to what follows, Urban Holzmeister, "Die Magdalenenfrage in der kirchlichen Überlieferung," *ZKT* 46 (1922): 402–22, 556–84; and Hans von Campenhausen, *The Virgin Birth in the Theology of the Ancient Church* (trans. F. Clarke; SHT 2; London: SCM, 1964), 45 n. 3. This tradition was especially strong in the early Syriac church: see Murray, *Symbols of Church and Kingdom*, 329–35.

the exception of the canonical gospels, however, the Christian literature of the first and early second centuries largely ignores both Mary of Magdala and Mary of Nazareth.[52] Consequently, many scholars have sought to resolve this issue with reference to Mary of Magdala's importance in the New Testament gospels, where the Magdalene is not only present at the crucifixion but in John's Gospel also receives the distinct honor of announcing Christ's resurrection to his followers. Some scholars conclude that these traditions clearly identify the gnostic Mary with the Magdalene rather than with Mary of Nazareth. Yet this criterion also fails to be decisive. Such argumentation neglects to consider that Mary of Nazareth is equally prominent in the canonical gospels and the Acts. Moreover, it does not take into account an early tradition, associated especially with ancient Syriac Christianity, that identifies Christ's mother, and not the Magdalene, as the first witness to the resurrection (discussed in the following section). This frequently ignored variant further complicates the identity of this puzzling figure.

In regard to the New Testament, it must be admitted that although Mary of Magdala does not appear very often, she is present at key moments in the Gospel narratives. Luke alone specifically notes her presence during Jesus' public ministry, mentioning her name in a list of women from whom Christ had cast out demons. These women, we are told, were following him and "provided for them out of their resources."[53] The other three Gospels, Matthew, Mark, and John, are united in recording the Magdalene's presence at the foot of the cross,[54] while Luke mentions only "the women who had followed him from Galilee."[55] Likewise, Matthew and Mark both note the Magdalene's presence at Jesus' burial,[56] and again Luke only refers to "the women who had come with him from Galilee."[57] John, on the other hand, fails to include any women at the burial, naming only

---

[52] "A part les Evangiles, les écrits chrétiens du Ier et du début du IIe siècle que j'appellerais, faute de mieux, orthodoxes, ignorent superbement notre disciple [Mary Magdalene]" (Bovon, "Le privilège pascal," 52); Hilda Graef, *Mary: A History of Doctrine and Devotion* (2 vols.; New York: Sheed & Ward, 1963), 1:33–34.

[53] Luke 8:1–3 (this and all other NT translations are taken from the NRSV, unless otherwise indicated); discussed in Atwood, *Mary Magdalene,* 11–41; and Carla Ricci, *Mary Magdalene and Many Others: Women Who Followed Jesus* (trans. P. Burns; Minneapolis: Fortress, 1994), passim.

[54] Matt 27:56; Mark 15:40; John 19:25; discussed by Atwood, *Mary Magdalene,* 43–66.

[55] Luke 23:49.

[56] Matt 27:61; Mark 15:47; Atwood, *Mary Magdalene,* 67–95.

[57] Luke 23:55.

Nicodemus and Joseph of Arimathea, the latter being the focus of all four accounts of Christ's burial.[58]

Perhaps Mary Magdalene's most important role, however, is as the first (or one of the first) to learn of Christ's resurrection.[59] All four Gospels identify Mary Magdalene as being among the first to discover and report the empty tomb. In the Synoptics, the Magdalene is accompanied by at least one other woman,[60] while in John she alone has the privilege of finding and announcing the empty tomb.[61] Neither Luke nor the shorter endings of Mark mention the risen Christ's appearance to the Magdalene, but in Matthew, Christ appears to both Mary Magdalene and "the other Mary," while John (along with the longer ending of Mark[62]) identifies Mary Magdalene alone as the first to behold the risen Christ.[63] While certain scholars have disputed the historicity of Christ's initial appearance to the Magdalene, on the basis of both Paul's account of the resurrection appearances in 1 Cor 15:5–8[64] and the contradictions among the various Gospel accounts,[65] the actuality of the event is for the present purpose irrelevant. The mere fact that many early Christians believed that Christ first appeared to the Magdalene is far more significant for determining exactly who might lurk behind the figure of the gnostic Mary.

On the basis of these traditions that Mary Magdalene (along with several other women) followed Christ in Galilee and figured prominently in the events of the passion and resurrection, several scholars have recently concluded that Mary of Magdala was a leader in the early Christian movement.[66]

---

[58] John 19:38–42.

[59] See the discussion of the different New Testament traditions in Atwood, *Mary Magdalene*, 97–146.

[60] Matt 28:1–10; Mark 16:1–8; Luke 24:1–11; also reported in *Gos. Pet.* 12 (Maria Grazia Mara, ed., *Évangile de Pierre: Introduction, texte critique, traduction, commentaire et index* [SC 201; Paris: Cerf, 1973], 62).

[61] John 20:1–2.

[62] Mark 16:9.

[63] John 20:10–18.

[64] "And that he appeared to Cephas, then to the twelve. Then he appeared to more than five hundred brothers and sisters at one time, most of whom are still alive, though some have died."

[65] See Bovon, "Le privilège pascal," 52; and the response to these in Elisabeth Schüssler Fiorenza, *Jesus, Miriam's Child, Sophia's Prophet: Critical Issues in Feminist Christology* (New York: Continuum, 1994), 119–28.

[66] See especially Elisabeth Schüssler Fiorenza, *In Memory of Her: A Feminist Theological Reconstruction of Christian Origins* (New York: Crossroad, 1985), 304–7, 323–33; more recently, King, "Gospel of Mary Magdalene," 2:618–20.

That Mary Magdalene may have had an important leadership role in the early Christian communities does not seem at all unlikely to me. But we must ask, does this rather attractive hypothesis necessarily translate into Mary of Magdala's equation with the gnostic Mary in the minds of early Christians or in modern interpretation? More specifically, is it sufficient to exclude certain other possibilities? I for one am not so persuaded. Were the Magdalene the only Mary portrayed in the New Testament as having participated in both Jesus' ministry and the early Christian community, then this line of reasoning would hold more force. But this is not the case: one must also, I propose, consider Mary of Nazareth, for whom there are similar indications.

The writings of the New Testament not only describe Mary of Nazareth's participation in events of her son's ministry and passion, but she is also identified as having been present in the company of the apostles for the beginnings of the Christian church. Of course, one might rightly object that the conflict between Christ and "his own" (οἱ παρ' αὐτοῦ) and then with his mother and brothers in Mark 3:20–35 makes Mary of Nazareth's actual participation in Christ's public ministry historically improbable; but this recognition is not especially relevant to the present question. As explained above with regard to Christ's appearance to the Magdalene, the probabilities of historical-critical New Testament scholarship are of little consequence for determining the identity of the gnostic Mary in the early Christian tradition. On the contrary, the aggregate of the Gospel traditions inherited by the early Christians is paramount in this instance, rather than a single passage set against the others. This precritical composite was the image of Mary of Nazareth that would have influenced the production and interpretation of stories about the gnostic Mary. Admittedly, Mark 3:20–35 presents an episode in which Christ distinguishes the members of his "eschatological family" from his biological family, suggesting his mother's separation from his ministry.[67] But looking at the totality of the canonical Gospel tradition(s), as they were (more or less) received by Christians of the second and third centuries, we see that Luke and John explicitly include Mary of Nazareth within Christ's "eschatological family,"[68] while Matthew softens Mark's exclusion.[69] Consequently, for our purposes, Mark 3:20–35 must be interpreted in light of these "facts," rather than against them, yielding an image of Mary of Nazareth in early Christianity as supportive of and occasionally a participant in her son's earthly ministry.

---

[67] "Eschatological family" is borrowed from Raymond E. Brown et al., eds., *Mary in the New Testament: A Collaborative Assessment by Protestant and Roman Catholic Scholars* (New York: Paulist, 1978), 51–59, where Mark 3:20–35 is discussed.

[68] See especially ibid., 213, 287–88.

[69] Ibid., 97–103.

Luke's Gospel especially nurtures this image, by developing the Virgin's role in the incarnation and emphasizing her willing participation in the process. Luke thus presents her not only as a member of Christ's eschatological family, but even as a model of discipleship, who at the annunciation is the first to hear and receive the word of God.[70] Luke portrays Mary of Nazareth as being "first and foremost a disciple of Jesus, ... but also a prophet," who in the Magnificat recalls the words of the prophets and foretells the themes of her son's preaching.[71] More importantly, Luke's second volume, the Acts of the Apostles, describes Mary of Nazareth's involvement in the nascent church.[72] Here Luke notes her presence among the apostles in the "Upper Room,"[73] and although she is not specifically identified as a leader, she is singled out among the other women present. The clear implication is that, after Christ's resurrection and ascension, Mary of Nazareth played a role in the formation of the Christian church (or at least, was reputed to have) and was in the company of the apostles as they began to preach the gospel, as a "founding mother" of the Jerusalem community.[74] This image seems to favor Mary of Nazareth's identification with the gnostic Mary. While Mary Magdalene is described as a participant in Jesus' public ministry and in the events of the passion and resurrection, there is no similar witness that she stood among the apostles after the resurrection and ascension and participated in the initial formation of the Christian church, as is the case with Mary of Nazareth. Since the gnostic Mary often appears similarly in the company of the apostles, after the ascension and discussing the gospel, Mary of Nazareth's comparable depiction in Acts might suggest to us, as well as to an ancient interpreter, that these two figures are identical.

Also suggestive of Mary of Nazareth's significance are her appearances in the Gospel of John, the very gospel that also presents some of the strongest evidence for the Magdalene's importance in earliest Christianity.[75] The first of these occurs at the wedding of Cana, an event that in John's Gospel inaugurates Jesus' public ministry.[76] Here Mary of

---

[70] Ibid., 125–26, 162–63.

[71] Beverly Roberts Gaventa, *Mary: Glimpses of the Mother of Jesus* (Columbia: University of South Carolina Press, 1995; repr., Minneapolis: Fortress, 1999), 73.

[72] Brown et al., *Mary in the New Testament,* 174–75.

[73] Acts 1:14.

[74] So Heikki Räisänen describes Mary of Nazareth's depiction in Acts as a part of the "Kernbestand der Jerusalemer Gemeinde": *Die Mutter Jesu im Neuen Testament* (2d ed.; STAT B/247; Helsinki: Suomalainen Tiedeakatemia, 1989), 141.

[75] Schüssler Fiorenza, *In Memory of Her,* 323–33; King, "Gospel of Mary Magdalene," 2:618–19.

[76] John 2:1–12.

Nazareth is not only present but influences her son to perform his first miracle, the transformation of water into wine. As Elisabeth Schüssler Fiorenza suggests, this story, which was a part of John's sign source, has probably been edited by the evangelist, who was uncomfortable with Mary's prominent role in the beginnings of Christ's ministry as found in his source. Consequently, Schüssler Fiorenza explains, the author of the Fourth Gospel has sought to minimize Mary of Nazareth's important role by inserting Jesus' rather puzzling reply to his mother: "Woman, what concern is that to you and to me? My hour has not yet come."[77] Nevertheless, despite this awkward response, Christ does in fact work the miracle that his mother requests, while she instructs the servants to do what he says. The overall effect of this incident is to connect Mary of Nazareth with Jesus' public ministry, both indicating her presence at its beginning and ascribing to her an important role in its activities: she persuades her son to commence his ministry with this miracle and gives the orders for its fulfillment. As the episode comes to a close, the Gospel further explains that "he went down to Capernaum with his mother, his brothers, and his disciples; and they remained there a few days."[78] This conclusion suggests that Mary of Nazareth's participation in her son's ministry, even if it was not continuous, was not limited to this event.[79] Clearly, then, Mary of Nazareth can rival the Magdalene's participation in Jesus' Galilean ministry, at least as she is portrayed in the Gospel traditions.

Finally, the Gospel of John shows Mary of Nazareth to have been, like the Magdalene, an important participant in the events of the passion.[80] While her absence in the Synoptic accounts is certainly important for historical-critical study, the early Christian tradition frequently harmonized the divergent accounts, identifying Mary of Nazareth with one of the

---

[77] Schüssler Fiorenza, *In Memory of Her,* 326–27; John 2:4.

[78] John 2:12.

[79] Brown et al., *Mary in the New Testament,* 196, conclude, "There is no reason in the Fourth Gospel, any more than in the Synoptic Gospels, to think that Mary was a disciple of Jesus during his ministry," but this judgment is based on historical-critical analysis of the text and especially thus represents an effort to subordinate other representations to the incident in Mark 3:20–35. While I would not dispute that from a historical-critical point of view this is a likely assessment of what "actually" happened in the first century, I maintain that in the absence of such criticism, the text would likely suggest a very different sort of "truth" to the Christians of the second and third (and subsequent) centuries. Indeed, the need felt by the interfaith committee that authored this volume to argue this point in its discussion of this passage seems to indicate that this is at some level an implication.

[80] John 19:25–27.

various "other Marys" mentioned by the Synoptic accounts.[81] Nevertheless, in contrast to the Synoptic versions, John's Gospel explicitly indicates Mary of Nazareth's presence beneath the cross, together with several other women, including Mary Magdalene, and the beloved disciple, whom later tradition would identify with John. From the cross, Jesus addresses both his mother and the beloved disciple, entrusting her to his care, in an action that, as one group of modern interpreters explains, "points to the future, the era of the disciples who will come after Jesus," thereby signaling her importance in this future.[82] By thus becoming the mother of the beloved disciple, who is "the disciple *par excellence*" in John's Gospel, Mary of Nazareth "becomes herself a model of belief and discipleship."[83] At the episode's conclusion the Gospel explains that Mary lived with the beloved disciple from that moment on. Since this figure was undoubtedly an important leader in the early church (traditionally, John),[84] one might well imagine that Mary of Nazareth accompanied the beloved disciple as he spread the gospel, and thus she was involved in the nascent church.[85] As with Mary's presence among the apostles in Acts, this too could suggest both to the modern and ancient interpreters alike that Mary of Nazareth was active in the beginnings of the Christian community, in a role not unlike the various depictions of the gnostic Mary.

While one must concede that historical-critical analysis of the New Testament makes rather likely that the "historical gnostic" Mary, if she existed, was in fact the Magdalene, this is ultimately outside the scope of the present study. Our concern instead is with how Christians of the late ancient period would have interpreted this Mary's identity. Even though the conflict between Jesus and his family described in Mark 3:20–35 makes Mary of Nazareth a

----

[81] Murray, *Symbols of Church and Kingdom,* 330–31, lists several such instances from the Syrian tradition, including the Syriac *Didascalia,* John Chrysostom, and Severus of Antioch. Jerome, however, without doubting Mary of Nazareth's presence at the cross, carefully distinguishes the Virgin from these other figures, in order to defend her perpetual virginity against the claims of Helvidius, who apparently conflated the different women: Jerome, *Helv.* 13–16 (PL 23:195–201). See also Claudia Setzer, "Excellent Women: Female Witness to the Resurrection," *JBL* 116 (1997): 260 n. 6; and Brown et al., *Mary in the New Testament,* 68–72, who on historical-critical grounds argue against any such identification.

[82] Brown et al., *Mary in the New Testament,* 288.

[83] Ibid., 289.

[84] Ibid., 211–12.

[85] This seems suggested especially by the later traditions of Mary's death at Ephesus, which, on the basis of this incident, suppose her to have accompanied John there as he was spreading the gospel. For more on these traditions, see the discussion in Mimouni, *Dormition,* 585–97.

rather unlikely candidate for the "historical gnostic" Mary, this passage alone cannot assure us that this is how Christians of the second, third, and fourth centuries would have interpreted this figure. The early church was not prone to reading with suspicion, ferreting out dissonances; rather, it read with fidelity, searching for consonance. With such a hermeneutic, Mary of Nazareth's involvement at the wedding in Cana, her presence at the cross, and her appearance among the apostles for the beginnings of the church in the Upper Room would very likely have led the early Christians to an altogether different conclusion regarding the identity of our apocryphal Mary.

3. Mary of Nazareth As Apostola Apostolorum in Early Christian Tradition

Despite the relatively equal importance of these two women in the writings of the New Testament, many will doubtless appeal to the risen Christ's appearance to the Magdalene at the close of the Fourth Gospel as favoring her identification as the gnostic Mary.[86] Christ's instruction in this Gospel that she announce his resurrection to the apostles, effectively making her an "*apostola apostolorum*," does indeed suggest an important role for the Magdalene in the early community. When combined with the apostles' skepticism at her report (in Luke and the longer ending of Mark), the Magdalene begins to look something like the gnostic Mary, who is often in conflict with certain of the apostles (especially Peter). Moreover, at least one scholar, Antti Marjanen, has added to this a claim that the risen Savior's appearance to his mother is unprecedented in early Christian literature, arguing that this makes unlikely Mary of Nazareth's identification with the gnostic Mary. The gnostic Mary frequently appears in conversation with the risen Christ, and while the Fourth Gospel offers precedent for Christ's appearance to the Magdalene, Marjanen maintains that there is no similar evidence for an early Christian tradition of Christ's appearance to his mother following the resurrection.[87] Marjanen's conclusions are somewhat overstated, however, and they depend very much on how one views the importance of certain data that suggest the contrary. As Enzo Lucchesi notes in his article, there is a well-attested patristic tradition of Christ's post-resurrection appearance to his mother. One can add to this a number of apocrypha (especially in Coptic), including the *Pistis Sophia,* for instance, where Mary of Nazareth is, together with the apostles, a privileged interlocutor in dialogues with her risen son.[88] Marjanen's argument is far too

---

[86] See, e.g., King, "Gospel of Mary Magdalene," 618.

[87] Marjanen, *The Woman Jesus Loved,* 94–95 n. 2.

[88] Enzo Lucchesi, "Évangile selon Marie ou Évangile selon Marie-Madeleine?" *AnBoll* 103 (1985): 366.

dismissive of this body of evidence, which can be seen as strongly supporting Mary of Nazareth's identification with the gnostic Mary.[89]

The most important component of this tradition is the early and influential tradition in the Syrian church that after his resurrection Christ appeared first to *his mother,* Mary of Nazareth, and not the Magdalene.[90] Although some uncertainty surrounds the origins of this tradition, it almost certainly dates back at least as far as Tatian's *Diatessaron,* composed sometime between 150 and 180.[91] This harmony of the four canonical gospels quickly displaced its sources to become the primary Gospel text of the Syrian church during the third and fourth centuries, after which time it was itself gradually supplanted by the four canonical gospels.[92] As a result of its displacement, no complete copy of the *Diatessaron* has survived,[93] and consequently its contents have to be determined indirectly, based largely on the testimony of several second- and third-hand witnesses. Only when a number of these converge can we obtain a high degree of certainty that a particular tradition was

---

[89] Antti Marjanen has continued to reject this evidence out of hand, without offering any explanation as to why. In both his book and in his response to my paper at the 2000 SBL Annual Meeting, he continues to insist that these traditions are late. Nevertheless, he has not yet explained this view. Although it may turn out that he is in fact correct, the current state of research strongly suggests otherwise. As demonstrated below in this article, according to the consensus procedures for identifying material from the *Diatessaron,* this variant shows every indication of originating in Tatian's Gospel harmony. If Professor Marjanen wishes to maintain otherwise, I would encourage him to explain his views.

[90] This is well discussed in Murray, *Symbols of Church and Kingdom,* 329–35.

[91] When one dates the *Diatessaron* depends a great deal on where and in what language one supposes it to have been composed. See the discussions in Arthur Vööbus, *Early Versions of the New Testament: Manuscript Studies* (PETSE 6; Stockholm: Estonian Theological Society in Exile, 1954), 1–6; Metzger, *Early Versions of the New Testament,* 30–32; William L. Petersen, "The Diatessaron of Tatian," in *The Text of the New Testament in Contemporary Research,* 77–96; and Carmel McCarthy, trans., *Saint Ephrem's Commentary on the Diatessaron* (Oxford: Oxford University Press, 1993), 3–7.

[92] Vööbus, *Early Versions of the New Testament,* 22–27; Louis Leloir, *Éphrem de Nisibe: Commentaire de l'évangile concordant ou Diatessaron* (SC 121; Paris: Cerf, 1966), 20; McCarthy, *Saint Ephrem's Commentary,* 7–8.

[93] According to a famous passage from Theodoret of Cyrrhus (d. 458), *Haereticarum fabularum compendium* 1.20 (PG 83:372A), two hundred of the eight hundred churches in his north-Syrian diocese were still using the *Diatessaron* instead of the separate Gospels. Theodoret put an end to this by rounding up and destroying these copies of the *Diatessaron* and replacing them with the four Gospels.

Stephen J. Shoemaker

present in the *Diatessaron,* and in the case of the risen Christ's appearance to his mother, we are fortunate that the assemblage of witnesses to this tradition is extraordinarily reliable.

Ephrem's commentary on the *Diatessaron* is one of the primary sources for knowledge of the *Diatessaron*'s contents, and this commentary is also a key witness to the tradition that the risen Christ appeared to his mother instead of the Magdalene. As Ephrem comments on Tatian's account of the empty tomb and the resurrection, he occasionally cites the *Diatessaron*'s text, which, as he reports it, apparently failed to identify the woman who discovers the tomb and sees the risen Christ as Mary Magdalene. Instead, she is known simply as "Mary." Then, when Ephrem comes to the passage describing Christ's postresurrection appearance to Mary, he ponders Christ's command that Mary not touch him, which he explains as follows: "Why, therefore, did he prevent Mary from touching him? Perhaps it was because he had confided her to John in his place, Woman, behold your son."[94] Thus the woman to whom Christ first appeared, the Magdalene in John's Gospel, is instead identified here as Christ's mother, whom he had entrusted to the care of his beloved disciple. Although some scholars were initially skeptical of this tradition, attributing it to Ephrem's interpretation rather than the text of the *Diatessaron,* for the most part its authenticity is now conceded.[95] The confluence of evidence from various sources has, for the most part, put this objection to rest, demonstrating with near certainty that this variant occurred in Tatian's harmony.[96]

A number of the best witnesses to the *Diatessaron*'s text confirm Ephrem's indication that Tatian's resurrection account did not specify the Magdalene's involvement, referring only to a woman named Mary. The first of these witnesses, the medieval Arabic translations of the *Diatessaron,* fail

---

[94] Ephrem, *Commentary on the Diatessaron* 21.27 (Louis Leloir, ed., Saint Éphrem, *Commentaire de l'évangile concordat: Texte syriaque [MS Chester Beatty 709]* [CBM 8; Dublin: Hodges Figgis, 1963], 228, translation from McCarthy, *Saint Ephrem's Commentary,* 331).

[95] Louis Leloir initially considered this to be Ephrem's invention but later changed his mind, at the influence of Robert Murray, and came to recognize the antiquity of this variant: Leloir, *Éphrem de Nisibe,* 75 n. 3. William L. Petersen notes the possibility that this variant is the work of Ephrem, yet without going so far as to dispute its authenticity in his *The Diatessaron and Ephrem Syrus As Sources of Romanos the Melodist* (CSCO 475, CSCO.Sub 74; Leuven: Peeters, 1985), 191, esp. n. 97.

[96] In addition to what follows, see Tjitze Baarda, *Aphrahat's Text of the Fourth Gospel* (vol. 1 of *The Gospel Quotations of Aphrahat the Persian Sage;* Amsterdam: Vrije Universiteit Amsterdam, 1975), 254–57, where this is quite thoroughly argued.

to identify this Mary in their reproduction of John 20:1–17. Then, following their report of Christ's appearance to "Mary" from John, the Arabic translations suddenly switch to Mark 16:9b, with which they introduce Mary Magdalene as if she were a completely different person from the woman to whom Christ first appeared.[97] Similar evidence is offered by the Old Syriac version of the Gospels, a second crucial witness to the text of the *Diatessaron*. These translations were probably realized during the second century, at approximately the same time that Tatian was composing his Gospel harmony, with which they have a close, if complicated, relationship.[98] No doubt because of the early dominance of the *Diatessaron*, which was followed by the establishment of the Peshitta version, the Old Syriac version is preserved by just two codices, both of which contain extensive fragments of the Gospels. Only one of these preserves sections of the Gospel of John, and we are fortunate that the conclusion has survived. This late fourth- or early fifth-century palimpsest from Sinai (one of the earliest manuscripts of the Gospels in any language)[99] agrees with Ephrem in naming the woman of John 20:11–18 simply as Mary and failing to identify her with the Magdalene.[100]

The relationships among Tatian's *Diatessaron*, the different Arabic versions of the *Diatessaron*, and the Old Syriac version are admittedly quite complex, but this assortment of witnesses is sufficient to assure us that this tradition almost certainly reaches back to Tatian. As Bruce Metzger explains:

> When one or more of these witnesses [MSS B E O of the Arabic *Diatessaron*] implies a Syriac text different from the Peshitta, particularly when such readings agree with the Old Syriac and/or with other Diatessaric

---

[97] A. S. Marmardji, ed., *Diatessaron de Tatien: Texte arabe établi, traduit en français, collationné avec les anciennes versions syriaques, suivi d'un évangéliaire diatessarique syriaque et accompagné de quatre planches hors texte* (Beirut: Imprimerie catholique, 1935), 508–10; see also Augustinus Ciasca, ed., *Tatiani evangeliorum harmoniae arabice* (Rome: Ex typographia polyglotta, 1888), ٢٠٠–٢٠١.

[98] The date of this translation is also complicated and depends primarily on how one understands the relation of the Old Syriac version to the *Diatessaron*, with which it is somehow linked. See the discussions in Vööbus, *Early Versions of the New Testament*, 73–88; and Metzger, *Early Versions of the New Testament*, 36–48, esp. 45–47.

[99] For the date, see Vööbus, *Early Versions of the New Testament*, 74; and Metzger, *Early Versions of the New Testament*, 38.

[100] Agnes Smith Lewis, *The Old Syriac Gospels or Evangelion da-mepharreshe* (London: Williams & Norgate, 1910), 264; F. Crawford Burkitt, *Evangelion da-mepharreshe* (2 vols.; Cambridge: Cambridge University Press, 1904), 1:528.

witnesses, we may with some measure of confidence regard such readings as genuine Tatianic remnants.[101]

Metzger later adds that "such a possibility becomes a probability with over-
whelming compulsion when Ephraem and other witnesses ... add their
support."[102] Such is the case with Christ's appearance to "Mary": it is
attested by the best Arabic manuscripts of the *Diatessaron,* the Old Syriac,
and Ephrem's commentary, making its presence in Tatian's harmony
extremely probable. This reading is further corroborated by a number of
early Syrian witnesses, as studies by Robert Murray and Tjitze Baarda have
shown, including the following: the Syriac *Didascalia,* the second pseudo-
Clementine *Epistle on Virginity,* John Chrysostom, Theodoret of Cyrrhus,
Jacob of Serug, Severus of Antioch, and the illuminations of the Syriac
Gospel Codex of Rabbula.[103] With this the authenticity of this tradition
draws near to certainty, and even on the slight chance that Tatian is not
himself its "originator," the impact of this reading on early Syrian Christianity is undeniable.

There is somewhat later evidence indicating that this tradition made an
impact elsewhere, including Egypt in particular.[104] Here the Magdalene's
identity was frequently merged with the Virgin, to whom the risen Christ
is also reported to have appeared. Many of these witnesses are admittedly

---

[101] Metzger, *Early Versions of the New Testament,* 17. Similar principles are
espoused by A. J. B. Higgins, "The Persian and Arabic Gospel Harmonies," in
*Studia Evangelica: Papers Presented to the International Congress on "The Four
Gospels in 1957" Held at Christ Church, Oxford, 1957* (ed. K. Aland et al.; TU
73; Berlin: Akademie-Verlag, 1959), 799; idem, "Tatian's Diatessaron and the
Arabic and Persian Harmonies," in *Studies in New Testament Language and
Text: Essays in Honour of George D. Kilpatrick on the Occasion of His Sixty-Fifth
Birthday* (ed. J. K. Elliott; Leiden: Brill, 1976), 255; A. Baumstark, review of
A. S. Marmardji, *Diatessaron de Tatien: Texte arabe établi, traduit en français,
collationné avec les anciennes versions syriaques, suivi d'un évangéliaire diatessarique syriaque et accompagné de quatre plances hors texte,* OrChr 33 (1936):
241–42; and Paul E. Kahle, *The Cairo Geniza* (2d ed.; New York: Praeger, 1960),
313.

[102] Metzger, *Early Versions of the New Testament,* 27.

[103] See Murray's discussion of these in *Symbols of Church and Kingdom,* 330–32;
Tjitze Baarda, "Jesus and Mary (John 20:16f.) in the Second Epistle on Virginity
Ascribed to Clement," in *Essays on the Diatessaron* (Kampen: Pharos, 1994),
87–110; R. H. Connolly, "Jacob of Serug and the Diatessaron," *JTS* 8 (1907): 581–90.

[104] See, e.g., C. Giannelli, "Témoignages patristiques grecs en faveur d'une
apparition du Christ ressuscité à la Vierge Marie," in *Mélanges M. Jugie, REByz* 11
(1953): 106–19.

more recent, including several "pseudopatristic" texts,[105] but there is also explicit testimony from several third-century apocrypha, namely the different apocryphal traditions associated with the apostle Bartholomew and, most importantly, the *Pistis Sophia*.[106] These texts, which figured in the discussion of the different names above, not only describe the risen Christ's appearance to his mother, but they also describe her involvement in discussions of the cosmic mysteries, as I have demonstrated elsewhere.[107]

In light of such evidence, Alfred Loisy went so far as to propose the possibility that John's Gospel originally placed Christ's mother, rather than the Magdalene, at the tomb and that this tradition was only later harmonized to agree with the Synoptics.[108] If this less than popular suggestion is somewhat unlikely, as Loisy himself was quick to concede,[109] it nevertheless seems quite possible that this may have been the form in which the Gospel first reached the Syrian East. Admittedly, however, the evidence does not demonstrate that Tatian's text explicitly identified Mary of *Nazareth* as the first to behold the risen Christ. It only indicates that in the earliest Syrian tradition this Mary's identity was unspecified. Nevertheless, I strongly agree with Tjitze Baarda (contra Schmidt et al.) that the failure of the early Syrian Gospel traditions to specify which Mary received the christophany would favor understanding the figure as Christ's mother, rather than Mary of Magdala, whose town of origin the Gospel traditions usually specify, in order to distinguish her from Mary (of Nazareth), for whom this is not the case.[110] This assumption is borne out by the studies of Baarda and Murray, which make clear that the early Syrian church did in fact identify this unspecified Mary with Mary of Nazareth, even if we

---

[105] See, e.g., nn. 48 and 49 above; see also P. Devos, "L'apparition du Resuscité à sa Mère: Un nouveau témoin copte," *AnBoll* 96 (1978): 388; idem, "De Jean Chrysostom à Jean de Lycopolis: Chrysostom et Chalkèdon," *AnBoll* 96 (1978): 389–403; and Eugène Revillout, *Évangile des douze apôtres* [PO 2/2; Paris: Librairie de Paris/Firmin-Didot et Cie, 1907), 182.

[106] In addition to the references in nn. 13 and 33 above, see also *The Coptic Gospel of Bartholemew:* Budge, *Coptic Apocrypha,* 12, 31–32, 42; Lacau, *Fragments d'apocryphes coptes,* 51. For the date of these Coptic traditions, see Schneemelcher, *New Testament Apocrypha,* 1:537; and Elliott, *Apocryphal New Testament,* 652.

[107] Shoemaker, "Rethinking the 'Gnostic Mary.'"

[108] Alfred Loisy, *Le quatrième évangile* (Paris: Alphonse Picard et Fils, 1903), 908 n. 1.

[109] Ibid. Nevertheless, Martin Albertz, "Über die Christophanie der Mutter Jesu," *TSK* 86 (1913): 483–516, argues in favor of this position at some length.

[110] Baarda, *Aphrahat's Text of the Fourth Gospel,* 486 n. 27, where he concludes that this is the correct interpretation of Tatian's text.

cannot be absolutely certain that this was determined by Tatian's harmony.[111] Consequently, there can no longer be any question of Ephrem having invented this tradition. Its diffusion among various late ancient sources confirms that it was undoubtedly well in place before Ephrem wrote his commentary on the *Diatessaron*. Exactly how long before, we cannot be certain, but the confluence of witnesses speaks strongly of its antiquity in the Syrian region.

4. Conclusions

In summary, then, the gnostic Mary's identity is by no means a simple matter, nor is her identification with Mary of Magdala as certain as it is frequently asserted in modern scholarship. The particular spelling of the name Mary is in no way a reliable criterion distinguishing the two women, even though this is the most frequently advanced argument in favor of the gnostic Mary's identity with Mary of Magdala. If anything, as we have seen, the spellings Mariam and Mariamme appear to favor an identification with Mary of Nazareth. Likewise, the writings of the New Testament fail to resolve this problem, since they show both Marys to have equally been important figures in early Christian memory. Even the Magdalene's role as *apostola apostolorum* in the Fourth Gospel does not tip the balance in her favor, since in early Christian Syria, where it seems most likely that the gnostic Mary traditions first developed, it was believed that Christ first appeared to his mother, Mary of Nazareth, commissioning her with a revelation to deliver to his followers. Moreover, apocryphal literature of early Christianity, including the Nag Hammadi texts and various other "gnostic" traditions, further indicate the gnostic Mary's connection with Mary of Nazareth, as I have argued in a separate article, which is really the second part of the present study.[112] Nevertheless, all of this is by no means intended to suggest that we now may simply identify Mary of Nazareth with the gnostic Mary, as was previously done in the Magdalene's case. Rather, we must proceed in our study of this curious, apocryphal woman with a caution that is nuanced by ambiguities present in what is in fact a composite figure, who draws both the Nazarene and the Magdalene into her identity.

---

[111] Murray, *Symbols of Church and Kingdom,* 329–35, is the best discussion of this issue, but see also Baarda, "Jesus and Mary"; idem, *Aphrahat's Text of the Fourth Gospel,* 254–57; and Walter Bauer, *Das Leben Jesu im Zeitalter der neutestamentlichen Apokryphen* (Tübingen: Mohr Siebeck, 1909), 263.

[112] Shoemaker, "Rethinking the 'Gnostic Mary.'"

The Mother of Jesus or the Magdalene? The Identity of Mary in the So-Called Gnostic Christian Texts

Antti Marjanen
University of Helsinki

When, more than ten years ago, I began to work on texts dealing with Mary in the so-called gnostic writings of the second and third centuries,[1] the research situation seemed pretty simple. Mary texts were taken to represent gnostic views characterized by great sympathy toward women and strong antipathy toward nongnostic "mainstream" Christians, who were pictured in these texts, especially through the figure of Peter, as hostile enemies of the female race. Based on these interpretations, stereotypical views received confirmation: gnostic movements adopted a favorable stand toward women's engagement in leadership roles in religious groups, whereas formative "mainstream" Christianity radically tended to limit female participation in the church.[2]

---

[1] Texts supposedly belonging to this group usually included the *Gospel of Thomas,* the *Sophia of Jesus Christ,* the *Dialogue of the Savior,* the *Gospel of Mary,* the *Gospel of Philip, Pistis Sophia,* the *Great Questions of Mary* (Epiphanius, *Pan.* 26.8.1–9.5), and some *Psalms of Heracleides* in the *Manichaean Psalm-Book;* the first to present and survey these texts was François Bovon in his important article "Le privilège pascal de Marie-Madeleine," *NTS* 30 (1984): 50–62. In addition to these so-called gnostic texts, Bovon also referred to the *Acts of Philip,* which he did not consider a gnostic writing, but which, according to him, served as an indication of the survival of gnostic Mary Magdalene traditions. Furthermore, after Bovon, it was assumed that the *First Apocalypse of James* should be counted among the so-called gnostic Mary Magdalene texts; see, e.g., Antti Marjanen, *The Woman Jesus Loved: Mary Magdalene in the Nag Hammadi Library and Related Documents* (Nag Hammadi and Manichaean Studies 40; Leiden: Brill, 1996), 131–32. For a different view, see Silke Petersen, *"Zerstört die Werke der Weiblichkeit!" Maria Magdalena, Salome und andere Jüngerinnen Jesu in christlich-gnostischen Schriften* (Nag Hammadi and Manichaean Studies 48; Leiden: Brill, 1999), 251.

[2] So, e.g., Elaine Pagels, *The Gnostic Gospels* (New York: Random House, 1981), 76–81; Robert M. Price, "Mary Magdalene: Gnostic Apostle?" *Grail* 6 (1990): 54–76; Renate Schmid, *Maria Magdalena in gnostischen Schriften* (Munich: Arbeitsgemeinschaft für Religions- und Weltanschauungsfragen, 1990).

During the course of studying the so-called gnostic Mary texts, I and others have found the picture becoming more complicated. For example, as a consequence of the discovery of the Nag Hammadi Library, the term Gnosticism has been redefined in various ways. Thus, some of the second- and third-century Mary texts that used to be called gnostic are no longer characterized as such.[3] For the sake of convenience, in this article I shall still call the second- and third-century Mary texts, mentioned in note 1, gnostic, although I shall add to it the attributive adjective "so-called" in order to underline the problematic character of the term. Besides, the careful analysis of Mary texts that were earlier considered gnostic shows that the schematic view of the controversy between Mary and the male disciples, reflected in the texts, cannot always be interpreted as an indication of a disagreement between gnostic and "mainstream" Christians over the position of women. In *Pistis Sophia,* for instance, the controversy seems to mirror an innergnostic dispute.[4] Thus, the claim that Gnosticism without exception held a positive attitude toward women and their participation in leadership roles in religious communities has proved to be an incorrect generalization. This is further corroborated by those Mary texts that, despite their highly appreciative view of Mary, can use pejorative terminology while speaking about women in general.[5]

While many features of the earlier consensus were shaken in the course of the 1990s, one thing remained untouched. Mary of the so-called gnostic texts was still identified as the Magdalene. But even this could not go unchallenged when the new century commenced. In his paper at the 2000 Society of Biblical Literature Meeting, Stephen Shoemaker presented a thesis that the Mary of the so-called second- and third-century gnostic texts—with the exception of some texts in the *Gospel of Philip* and *Pistis Sophia*—was not the Magdalene but the mother of Jesus.[6] Shoemaker's thesis presupposes

---

[3] After finishing my own work on the so-called gnostic Mary texts (Marjanen, *The Woman Jesus Loved*), I have redefined my conception of Gnosticism such that I no longer regard the *Gospel of Thomas,* the *Dialogue of the Savior,* and the *Gospel of Mary* as gnostic. Even if the anthropology and the soteriology of these writings correspond to that of Gnosticism (or Platonism) with the emphasis on the return of the preexistent soul to the realm of light as a sign of ultimate salvation, none of these writings contains the other central feature of Gnosticism. They do not contain the idea of a cosmic world created by an evil and/or ignorant demiurge.

[4] See Marjanen, *The Woman Jesus Loved,* 179–84; Petersen, *"Zerstört die Werke der Weiblichkeit!"* 182–88.

[5] See Marjanen, *The Woman Jesus Loved,* 220–21.

[6] Stephen J. Shoemaker, "Rethinking the 'Gnostic Mary': Mary of Nazareth and Mary of Magdala in Early Christian Tradition" (paper presented at the Annual Meeting of the Society of Biblical Literature in Nashville, Tenn., November 2000; see Schoemaker's

that the Dormition texts, which were not composed until the beginning of the fifth century, contain earlier traditions that depict the Virgin Mary in the same way as the second- and third-century so-called gnostic texts.[7] The purpose of this article is to give a critical assessment of this thesis.

In support of his case, Shoemaker presents three arguments. The first has to do with the way the name Mary is written in each particular case either in Greek or in Coptic. Earlier it had been argued, for example, by myself, that especially in the so-called gnostic texts where Mary is explicitly characterized as the mother of Jesus the name is spelled *maria*.[8] Therefore it has been asserted that, when another version of the name, *mariham(mē)*, is employed, then Mary Magdalene is meant. There is a concrete and an explicit example of the use of the latter name in *Pistis Sophia* 124.11–13,[9] where, in the course of the dialogue, Jesus praises "the other Mary" for her thoughtful interpretation of his speech and calls her *mariham*. The context makes it fully clear that "the other Mary" cannot be the mother of Jesus; rather, she has to be Mary Magdalene. On the other hand, when Mary is explicitly introduced as the mother of Jesus in this section, the name is always written *maria* (116.21–22, 25–26; 117.21; 120.14, 19; 123.5–6; 124.6, 14, 19; 125.15).[10] This indeed suggests that, at least in *Pistis Sophia, mariham* seems to be the form of the name connected with the Magdalene and not with the Virgin Mary.

Nevertheless, Shoemaker is right when he insists that there are second- and third-century Greek texts in which *mariam* or *mariammē* is used for the mother of Jesus. In addition, Shoemaker correctly emphasizes that even the Sahidic translation of the New Testament can employ a form of the name *mariham* when speaking about the mother of Jesus (Matt 13:55). In light of

---

contribution in this volume). With regard to Mary in the *Gospel of Mary*, it was already suggested earlier that she should be identified with Mary of Nazareth rather than with Mary of Magdala; see Enzo Lucchesi ("Évangile selon Marie ou Évangile selon Marie-Madeleine?" *AnBoll* 103 [1985]: 366) in his review of Michel Tardieu's book *Écrits gnostiques: Codex de Berlin* (Sources gnostiques et manichéennes 1; Paris: Cerf, 1984). A similar suggestion is made by Philip Sellew, "An Early Coptic Witness to the *Dormitio Mariae* at Yale: P.CtYBR inv. 1788 Revisited," *BASP* 37 (2000): 52 n. 43.

[7] The conjecture that the texts contain earlier traditions is based on the ideas that these Dormition texts preserve traces of gnostic influence, especially in the form of the demiurge, and of early angel Christology (see n. 14 below).

[8] Marjanen, *The Woman Jesus Loved*, 63–64.

[9] For the text and an English translation of *Pistis Sophia*, see Carl Schmidt, ed., *Pistis Sophia* (trans. V. MacDermot; NHS 9; Leiden: Brill, 1978). In the present article, the references to *Pistis Sophia* are made according to this work. The first number gives the page number of the Coptic text, the second number refers to the line.

[10] The same is true with *Pistis Sophia* 13.13, which is the only other passage in the entire writing where Mary, explicitly characterized as the mother of Jesus, occurs.

this, it has to be admitted that, generally speaking, the use of the name *mari-ham(mē)* is not a conclusive argument for maintaining that in instances where this particular form of the name is used it must refer to Mary Magdalene. On the other hand, one cannot close one's eyes to the fact that at least in the so-called second- and third-century gnostic texts it is much more common to style the mother of Jesus *maria* than *mariham(mē)*, whereas the latter form of the name is used relatively often for Mary Magdalene.

The second argument Shoemaker advances for his thesis is that the apocryphal Mary of Nazareth traditions, especially the so-called Dormition and Assumption texts, as well as the Mandaean texts, contain features in their descriptions of the mother of Jesus similar to the so-called gnostic texts when they speak about a Mary, traditionally interpreted to be the Magdalene. As far as the Mandaean texts are concerned, I have no difficulty accepting that Miriai of the Mandaean texts is to be identified with or at least derives its origin from Mary of Nazareth.[11] But I do find it unlikely that the Mary of the so-called gnostic texts is to be identified with Miriai in the Mandaean texts. The connections are simply too general or too distant to prove this linkage. The fact that Miriai is portrayed as a "proto-convert" to or a "founding mother" of Mandaeism or that she carried out a "priestly function"[12] does not necessarily suggest that she has to be, or not even that she is most likely to be, identical with the so-called gnostic Mary. In a more detailed comparison between the Mandaean Miriai and the so-called gnostic Mary texts, there are no common features that would point to a common background behind these traditions. Even the fact that Miriai must defend her new-found faith before important religious male leaders, which of course in a very broad sense is comparable to the situation of Mary in the so-called gnostic texts, cannot warrant the conclusion that there is a real parallel between them, since the male leaders in the Mandaean texts are Miriai's own father and the Jewish leaders, whereas in the so-called gnostic texts Mary's opponents are Jesus' male disciples.

As to the Dormition texts, Shoemaker's case is more challenging. His claim that Mary in those writings is identical with the so-called gnostic Mary is based on the "Palm of the Tree of Life" traditions found in the Dormition and Assumption apocrypha[13] in which the Virgin Mary is instructed

---

[11] So convincingly Jorunn Jacobson Buckley, "The Mandaean Appropriation of Jesus' Mother, Miriai," *NovT* 35 (1993): 181–96. For a translation of the text, see Mark Lidzbarski, *Das Johannesbuch der Mandäer* (Giessen: Töpelmann, 1915), 126–38.

[12] The expressions used by Shoemaker to depict the Mandaean Miriai derive from the analysis by Buckley, "Mandaean Appropriation."

[13] For recent helpful introductions to various Dormition and Assumption apocrypha, see Stephen J. Shoemaker, "Mary and the Discourse of Orthodoxy: Early

by the Savior, the Great Angel, to communicate hidden mysteries to the apostles. Among these mysteries, there is a secret prayer that helps the souls to ascend from this world past its demiurge, who is portrayed as "a beast with the body of a lion and the tail of the snake," to their true home with God in the fullness. This gnostic theme, which is linked to the Dormition apocrypha and which according to Shoemaker can be traced back to the second or third century,[14] has also led him to conclude that the Mary of the so-called second- and third-century gnostic texts does not need to be the Magdalene but is the Virgin Mary.

Although there is no conflict between Mary of Nazareth and the male disciples in these particular versions of the Dormition legend, it undeniably contains some other features that bring to mind the so-called gnostic Mary, especially in the *Manichaean Psalm-Book* and in the *Gospel of Mary*. In the *Manichaean Psalm-Book* (187),[15] Mary is entrusted by the risen Jesus with the task of bringing a special message to the male disciples of Jesus, although the message does not contain any secrets but is an invitation to return to the risen Savior. Besides, the particular psalm that tells about the assignment of Mary is clearly dependent on John 20:11–18[16] and thus gives good reason for identifying the protagonist of the text with the Magdalene and not with the mother of Jesus. In the *Gospel of Mary,* however, Mary gives her male colleagues a special revelation, imparted by the Savior (10.7–17.9),[17] which contains a description of a soul's ascent to the rest and can thus serve as an instruction as to how to get past various dangers

---

Christian Identity and the Ancient Dormition Legends" (Ph.D. diss., Duke University, 1997); and Sellew, "Early Coptic Witness," 37–69.

[14] The identification of the Savior with the Great Angel is also seen by Shoemaker as an early feature in the text.

[15] For the text and a translation, see C. R. C. Allberry, *A Manichaean Psalm-Book: Part II* (Manichaean Manuscripts in the Chester Beatty Collection 2; Stuttgart: Kohlhammer, 1938). In this article, all the references are made according to this work. The first number gives the page number of the Coptic text, and the second number refers to the line.

[16] For the arguments, see Marjanen, *The Woman Jesus Loved,* 206–8. Shoemaker has suggested that there is an early Syrian tradition that has interpreted John 20:11–18 in such a way that it is not Mary Magdalene but the Virgin Mary who experiences the first appearance of the Risen One. It is not at all clear, however, whether the replacement of Mary Magdalene with the mother of Jesus, which does occur in the Syrian interpretation of John 20:11–18, is as early as Shoemaker suggests; for this, see Marjanen, *The Woman Jesus Loved,* 94–95.

[17] For the text, see Robert McL. Wilson and George W. MacRae, "BG,1: The Gospel according to Mary," in *Nag Hammadi Codices V,2–5 and VI with Papyrus Berolinensis 8502,1 and 4* (ed. D. M. Parrott; NHS 11; Leiden: Brill, 1979), 453–71.

on the way to the realm of light.[18] Does the *Gospel of Mary* provide such a link between the so-called gnostic Mary and the Mary of the Dormition apocrypha that can be used to establish a common identity between the Marys in the way Shoemaker has done? Since Mary in the *Gospel of Mary* does not have any epithet that would identify her more closely, it seems possible at first sight to regard her as the mother of Jesus. However, there are other features in the *Gospel of Mary* that link the protagonist of the text more closely to the Magdalene than to Mary of Nazareth. But I shall return to this question after I have discussed Shoemaker's third argument, since it bears on the interpretation of Mary in the *Gospel of Mary*.

The third argument Shoemaker advances in support of his thesis has to do with *Pistis Sophia,* which is one of those so-called gnostic writings that displays a conflict between Mary and the male disciples, especially Peter. As we have noted earlier, in this text it is explicitly stated that among the interlocutors of the Savior there are two Marys, the Magdalene and the mother of Jesus. Shoemaker argues that the one who comes into conflict with Peter is not the Magdalene but Mary of Nazareth. He comes to this conclusion by pointing out that when Mary is introduced into the text for the first time and presents an interpretation of a speech of the Savior, she is congratulated by him as follows: "You are blessed among all women on earth" (28.21–22).[19] Later on, as this Mary continues to interpret the speeches of the Savior, he praises her: "Mariam, you blessed one ... who will be called blessed by all generations" (56.11–13). According to Shoemaker these congratulations are clear allusions to the Lukan birth narrative and show that the Mary in these passages and in most parts of *Pistis Sophia*—with the exception of those references where Mary is explicitly styled the Magdalene—has to be the mother of Jesus. Thus, she is also the one who collides with Peter in *Pistis Sophia* 58.11–14, 162.14–18.

---

[18] Because of its fragmentary nature, it is difficult to say with certainty whether the *Gospel of Mary* has included a passage in which the soul meets a demiurge-like figure. This is not likely, however, since this kind of meeting should probably have taken place before the final deliverance of the soul from the bondage of the world. In the *Gospel of Mary* the entry of the soul into the realm of light is nevertheless preceded by an encounter between the soul and the seven powers of wrath, during which the soul presents such an answer to the questions of the powers that she is released from their hands (16.12–17.4).

[19] Already in *Pistis Sophia* 26.12 a Mary asks the permission of the Savior to present an interpretation of his words. It is interesting that in this passage the Coptic version of the name is *mariham,* whereas in 28.20 when she finishes her speech and is called "blessed among all women on earth," her name is spelled *maria;* for the different spelling of the name and its significance, see below.

The matter is not so simple, however. Basically, there are three kinds of Mary texts in the first three books of *Pistis Sophia:*[20] those explicitly connected with the mother of Jesus, those explicitly linked with Mary Magdalene, and a great number of texts that refer to a Mary (*maria, mariham,* or *marihammē*) without specifying more precisely who is meant. The important question is of course how these nonspecified references are to be explained. Shoemaker's attempt to use the text of the Lukan birth narrative as an interpretive key is not convincing. To be sure, Jesus says to his mother, "You will be blessed to the ends of the earth" (117.22–23), but in the entire section (116.21–126.18) in which both Mary of Nazareth and "the other Mary," who has to be the Magdalene, are introduced together it is not the mother of Jesus but the Magdalene who receives the epithet "the blessed one" (116.25–117.2, 120.11–16).[21] This epithet is also repeated later. As we have noted above, it is furthermore important to realize that in all those instances in *Pistis Sophia* in which Mary is explicitly identified as the mother of Jesus her name is never spelled in any other way than *maria.* "The other Mary," the Magdalene, is frequently written *mariham* as well. Thus, in the passage in which Peter attacks a Mary "because (he is) not able to suffer this woman who takes the opportunity (from him)," it is *mariham,* the blessed one, that is, Mary Magdalene, whom he is talking about.[22] Based on these observations, it is difficult to argue that the most important female protagonist of *Pistis Sophia* is the mother of Jesus and not the Magdalene. Thus, the figure of Mary in *Pistis Sophia* does not force us to reevaluate the identity of Mary in the related texts either.

Before a final appraisal of Shoemaker's thesis can be undertaken, I shall return to the question of the identity of Mary in the *Gospel of Mary.* At the same time it gives me an opportunity to summarize the arguments on the basis of which I myself still hold to the traditional identification of Mary as the Magdalene in the so-called second- and third-century gnostic texts. As stated above, Mary in the *Gospel of Mary* and the Virgin Mary in the "Palm of the Tree of Life" traditions found in the Dormition and Assumption apocrypha have some similarities, especially the fact that Mary is presented as an instructor of the male disciples in the secret mysteries

---

[20] The fourth book has been only secondarily attached to the rest of the writing (for this see, Marjanen, *The Woman Jesus Loved,* 170–73) and does not need to be taken into account here.

[21] It is to be noted that even the entire group of the disciples can be called "blessed beyond all human beings upon earth" (15.16–17). Thus, a reference to a person "being blessed" need not reflect a conscious influence of Lukan emphases at all; the state of blessedness is simply a common way to describe Christian life.

[22] See also *Pistis Sophia* 162.12–163.13.

imparted by the risen Savior and that she also gives them guidance as to how to manage the ascent to the heavenly realm. In these similarities one can see an indication that the *Gospel of Mary* could contain a version of a Mary tradition that has been integrated into later Dormition texts, and, thus, one could think that Mary in the *Gospel of Mary,* who is in no way speci-fied, is Mary of Nazareth and not the Magdalene.

This assumption has two problems. First of all, it does not take into account the possibility that the authors or redactors of Dormition texts could also have used a piece of Mary tradition, originally not related to the Virgin Mary but to another Mary, the Magdalene, for example, and appropriated it in a new context. There are plenty of indications that the different Marys of early Christianity and traditions connected with them were being conflated during the early centuries.[23] Therefore, it is not self-evident that, if certain features are connected with the Virgin Mary in fifth-century writings (even though they can contain earlier traditions as well), then similar features linked to a nonspecified Mary in a second-century text have to be interpreted such that the latter Mary must be identical with the mother of Jesus.

The second problem with the assumption that Mary in the *Gospel of Mary* is the mother of Jesus has to do with the fact that not only does the text share some common features with Dormition apocrypha, but it also has even closer similarities to the so-called second- and third-century gnos-tic Mary texts. As to the precise identity of Mary, it is interesting to note that the *Gospel of Mary* has the most conspicuous parallels to those texts that explicitly refer to Mary Magdalene. In the *Gospel of Philip,*[24] Mary Mag-dalene is introduced as the disciple Jesus loved more than all the (male) disciples (63.30–64.9). Since the same motif of Jesus' special love for Mary also appears in the *Gospel of Mary* (18.14–15) and since in both Gospels this fact arouses great annoyance among the male disciples, it is difficult

---

[23] A typical illustration of this is the way the different anointment accounts of the New Testament Gospels (see Urban Holzmeister, "Die Magdalenenfrage in der kirchlichen Überlieferung," *ZKT* 46 [1922]: 402–22, 556–84) and the appearance story in John 20:11–18 (see note 16) were interpreted by various church fathers. For the processes whereby the roles assigned to Mary Magdalene are transferred to the mother of Jesus, see also Ann Graham Brock, "Authority, Politics, and Gen-der: Mary, Peter, and the Portrayal of Leadership" (Ph.D. diss., Harvard Divinity School, 2000).

[24] For the text and an English translation, see Bentley Layton and Wesley W. Isenberg in *Gospel according to Thomas, Gospel according to Philip, Hypostasis of the Archons, and Indexes* (vol. 1 of *Nag Hammadi Codex II,2–7 together with XIII,2*, Brit. Lib. Or. 4926[1], and P. Oxy. 1, 654, 655;* ed. B. Layton; NHS 20; Lei-den: Brill, 1989), 142–215.

to avoid the impression that not only in the *Gospel of Philip* but also in the *Gospel of Mary* Mary Magdalene is portrayed as the beloved disciple of Jesus. The impression is bolstered by the fact that the tension between the male disciples and Mary Magdalene is also a central theme in *Pistis Sophia,* in which Mary Magdalene also appears to be Jesus' most favored disciple.[25] In all three of these texts Mary must undeniably be the Magdalene.

In six other second- and third-century so-called gnostic Mary texts her identity is never explicitly defined. But even if the form of the name is not taken into account it is most likely that in each case she is to be identified as the Magdalene. With regard to *Gos. Thom.* 114,[26] this becomes clear once it is realized that the text is characterized by a similar tension between Mary and the male disciples, especially Peter, which is found in all the three writings mentioned above. As stated already, the most important Mary text in the *Manichaean Psalm-Book* follows John 20:11–18 so closely that her identification with the Magdalene is self-evident. There are two other texts in the *Psalms of Heracleides* of the *Manichaean Psalm-Book* in which Mary appears. Both of them are part of a catalogue of disciples (192.5–193.3; 194.7–22) that lists both Jesus' male apostles and female followers with a short characterization of each. In 192.21–22 Mary is described as "a net-caster ... hunting for the eleven others that were lost." This description connects her with the psalm on page 187, which contains a similar depiction of Mary and presents a Manichaean appropriation of John 20:11–18 and thus makes it obvious that the woman in each Mary text of the *Manichaean Psalm-Book* is the Magdalene. In the lists of disciples included in the *Manichaean Psalm-Book,* Mary (i.e., the Magdalene) is accompanied by several other women, including Martha, Salome, and Arsinoe. The same four women appear in the *First Apocalypse of James*[27] (40.25–26[28]), which suggests that Mary is also the Magdalene in that text.

The conjecture that Mary in the two remaining revelation dialogues, the *Sophia of Jesus Christ* and the *Dialogue of the Savior,*[29] is also the Magdalene

---

[25] See my remarks above; for a more thorough treatment of Mary Magdalene in *Pistis Sophia,* see Marjanen, *The Woman Jesus Loved,* 170–88.

[26] For the text and an English translation of the *Gospel of Thomas,* see Bentley Layton and Thomas O. Lambdin in *Gospel according to Thomas, Gospel according to Philip, Hypostasis of the Archons, and Indexes,* 52–93.

[27] For the text and an English translation, see W. R. Schoedel, "NHC V,3: The (First) Apocalypse of James," in *Nag Hammadi Codices V,2–5 and VI with Papyrus Berolinensis 8502,1 and 4* (ed. D. M. Parrott; NHS 11; Leiden: Brill, 1979), 65–103.

[28] For the reconstruction of the text, see Marjanen, *The Woman Jesus Loved,* 132–35.

[29] For the texts and English translations, see Douglas M. Parrott, ed., *Nag Hammadi Codices III,3–4 and V,1 with Papyrus Berolinensis 8502,3 and Oxyrhynchus*

basically depends on the similarity of the genre to those Mary texts in which the identification is more obvious. As in *Pistis Sophia* and the *Gospel of Mary,* Mary Magdalene is thus presented as an interlocutor of Jesus together with other disciples during a dialogue that takes place after the resurrection and before the ascension of Jesus. Admittedly, the evidence for the assumption is not very strong,[30] but an attempt to view Mary in these texts as the mother of Jesus lies on still weaker grounds. Apart from the first three books of *Pistis Sophia,* in which Mary the mother of Jesus has a relatively insignificant role, she does not appear among the interlocutors in the revelation dialogues between the Risen Jesus and his disciples.[31]

The last of the nine so-called gnostic Mary texts is the *Great Questions of Mary,* an excerpt of which is summarized in Epiphanius, *Panarion.*[32] The text narrates an episode during which the Savior takes Mary to a mountain, copulates there with a woman pulled forth from his own side, partakes of his own emission, and finally instructs Mary, who has been watching the incident, that this is the way the future gnostics should do. This ritual act is seen as a kind of eucharistic meal, the purpose of which is to prevent the souls, hidden in male emission, from being imprisoned in human bodies.[33] It is not altogether clear which Mary Epiphanius or the author of the *Questions of Mary* have in mind while writing the text. The fact that just a bit earlier Epiphanius had mentioned the mother of Jesus and called her "the ever-virgin Mary" (*Pan.* 26.7.5), while he later makes no effort to connect her with the episode he is describing suggests that Mary in this text is not Mary of Nazareth but the Magdalene. The dearth of the epithet is not surprising, since Epihanius omits it elsewhere even when he undeniably refers to Mary Magdalene (see *Pan.* 26.15.6).

Papyrus 1081: Eugnostos and the Sophia of Jesus Christ (NHS 27; Leiden: Brill, 1991); and Stephen Emmel, ed., *Nag Hammadi Codex III,5: The Dialogue of the Savior* (NHS 26; Leiden: Brill, 1984).

[30] To be sure, both writings utilize that Coptic version of Mary's name (*mariham[mēi]*) which is commonly used for the Magdalene and very seldom for the mother of Jesus in the second- and third-century Coptic texts.

[31] In a third-century revelation dialogue, the *Questions of Bartholomew,* Mary the mother of Jesus is not really counted among the disciples as a member of their group, but she clearly appears as a kind of independent figure in the text. For an English translation of the text, see F. Scheidweiler in *Gospels and Related Writings* (vol. 1 of *New Testament Apocrypha;* ed. W. Schneemelcher; trans. R. McL. Wilson; rev. ed.; Cambridge: Clarke; Louisville: Westminster John Knox, 1991), 537–57.

[32] For the text and an English translation, see Marjanen, *The Woman Jesus Loved,* 191–94.

[33] For a more detailed analysis of the text, see ibid., 197–99.

Despite the many intriguing challenges Shoemaker's paper issues it is difficult to avoid the impression that the Dormition apocrypha do not provide a new key to the interpretation of Mary in the so-called second- and third-century gnostic texts. In light of the observations presented above, the traditional understanding according to which Mary in these so-called gnostic writings is the Magdalene is still most likely.[34]

---

[34] This does not mean that elements of the picture of Mary Magdalene remain unchangeable during the process of transmission. For example, in the *Manichaean Psalm-Book* Mary (Magdalene) is introduced as Martha's sister (192.23). The statement seems to derive from the period when at least the figures of Mary Magdalene and Mary of Bethany began to be fused together.

Setting the Record Straight—The Politics of Identification: Mary Magdalene and Mary the Mother in *Pistis Sophia*

Ann Graham Brock
Iliff School of Theology

Discerning the identity of a particular Mary in various ancient Christian texts has recently become the topic of increased debate, as even the existence of this volume testifies. Adding fuel to the fire of the controversy are the frequency and abundance of figures named Mary in early Christian texts, including Mary Magdalene, Mary the mother of Jesus, Mary of Bethany, and Mary of Clopas, to name a few. Of all the Marys, the two figures most frequently making an appearance in these ancient texts are, of course, Mary Magdalene and Mary the mother of Jesus. The issue at hand is the problem raised by the occasions in which a primary figure in the text is named Mary but is not otherwise more specifically identified. Are scholars correct to interpret this character so often as Mary Magdalene?

Certain scholars such as Enzo Lucchesi and Stephen J. Shoemaker would answer this question with a resounding no. They instead call this frequent identification of Mary as Mary Magdalene into question, rejecting what they consider to be an identification of Mary Magdalene that is too facile and fails to give Mary the Mother her due.[1] Shoemaker, for instance,

---

[1] Enzo Lucchesi, "Évangile selon Marie ou Évangile selon Marie-Madeleine?" *AnBoll* 103 (1985): 366; Stephen J. Shoemaker, "Mary and the Discourse of Orthodoxy: Early Christian Identity and the Ancient Dormition Legends" (Ph.D. diss., Duke University, 1997). Shoemaker's dissertation and subsequent research on the Dormition texts has contributed to the current knowledge concerning Mary of Nazareth, mother of Jesus, especially as he has made some of these texts available online. He builds in part upon Robert Murray's work on the early Syrian church and the tradition therein that Christ first appeared to his mother rather than Mary Magdalene. See Robert Murray, *Symbols of Church and Kingdom: A Study in Early Syriac Tradition* (Cambridge: Cambridge University Press, 1975). Although Shoemaker states that Lucchesi "briefly argued" that scholars have too hastily removed the Virgin from consideration (Shoemaker, "Mary and the Discourse of Orthodoxy,"

states, "Although scholars have repeatedly identified this Mary exclusively with the Magdalene rather than the Virgin, this interpretive dogma is based on evidence" he evaluates as "at best inconclusive."[2] He argues instead, "In both the *Gospel according to Mary* and the *Pistis Sophia,* the evidence favoring an identification of this 'gnostic' Mary with the Virgin is actually quite strong and has unfortunately been overlooked by students of early Christian apocrypha."[3] The object of this essay, therefore, is to take his challenge seriously and once again review the literary evidence. Since Karen King provides the primary argumentation for identifying the unnamed Mary in the *Gospel of Mary* as Mary Magdalene, I will focus instead upon the other text Shoemaker calls into question: *Pistis Sophia.* The results of my research will indicate that at least with respect to *Pistis Sophia* 1–3 there is indeed strong justification for believing that the primary figure is Mary Magdalene and not Mary the Mother, as Shoemaker suggests.

1. Mary and Mary in Pistis Sophia *1–3 and* Pistis Sophia *4*

This essay begins with an essential first step of nuancing the discussion concerning the text called *Pistis Sophia* by not treating it as a homogenous unity, as so frequently occurs. What is now called *Pistis Sophia* was apparently comprised of two originally independent texts: *Pistis Sophia* 1–3, frequently dated to the second half of the third century, and *Pistis Sophia* 4, dated slightly earlier to the first half of the third century, according to Harnack and others.[4] For the purposes of this essay, evidence of further

---

173), I would not characterize Lucchesi's points as a brief argument, as he does not provide much justification but something more akin to a claim.

[2] Shoemaker, "Mary and the Discourse of Orthodoxy," 171.

[3] Stephen J. Shoemaker, "Rethinking the 'Gnostic Mary': Mary of Nazareth and Mary of Magdala in the Gospel of Mary," *Society of Biblical Literature 2000 Abstracts* (Atlanta: Society of Biblical Literature, 2000), 92.

[4] Marjanen provides some good discussion concerning the dating of these texts, stating that it is difficult to date the two texts with respect to each other based on the observations of Schmidt. See Antti Marjanen, *The Woman Jesus Loved: Mary Magdalene in the Nag Hammadi Library and Related Documents* (Nag Hammadi and Manichaean Studies 40; Leiden: Brill, 1996), 171–72, esp. 172 n. 11. Previous work on this topic in Adolf von Harnack, *Untersuchungen über das gnostische Buch 'Pistis Sophia'* (TU 7; Leipzig: Hinrichs, 1891), 106–12. See also his "Ein jüngst entdeckter Auferstehungsbericht," in Caspar René Gregory et al., *Theologische Studien: Herrn Wirkl. Oberkonsistorialrath Professor D. Bernhard Weiss zu seinem 70. Geburtstage* (Göttingen: Vandenhoeck & Ruprecht, 1897), 1. Other scholars, such as Carl Schmidt and Walter Till, agree with Harnack's dating of these two sections: Carl Schmidt, *Pistis Sophia: Ein gnostisches Originalwerk des 3. Jahrhunderts aus dem Koptischen übersetzt* (Leipzig: Hinrichs, 1925), xl–lxxxi; idem, "Die Urschrift der

layering of traditions and rewritings of this composite text will not be explored beyond these two larger divisions.

It is not surprising that the following statistics concerning the variations of the forms of the names of Mary serve to confirm the need to treat these two texts of *Pistis Sophia* separately. *Pistis Sophia* 4, for instance, presents only one Mary and uses only one form of her name. Moreover, the identity of this Mary in *Pistis Sophia* 4 is more difficult to discern than in *Pistis Sophia* 1–3 because there are no specific indicators or additional phrases to help specify this Mary as either Mary Magdalene or Mary the Mother. Interestingly, the most frequent female form of Mary (**ⲘⲀⲢⲒⲀ**) in *Pistis Sophia* 1–3 (that is, "Maria") never occurs once in *Pistis Sophia* 4. Instead every reference to the primary figure of *Pistis Sophia* 4 employs only the name **ⲘⲀⲢⲒ2ⲀⲘ** ("Mariam"), apparently referring to only one character. Although the name Mariam appears proportionately less frequently than in *Pistis Sophia* 1–3, it nevertheless still appears eight times (in chs. 138, 139, 144, 145, 146, and 148), a ratio significantly higher than all the other disciples. Additionally, a large lacuna must have had at least one more reference to Mary, as the text states, "Mariam continued again and said . . ." (*Pistis Sophia* 4.144).[5] The use of her name thus exceeds all other disciples (with four references to Thomas, two to Andrew, Bartholomew, Philip, Peter, and John, and only one to James, Simon the Canaanite, Philip, and Salome).

By contrast, *Pistis Sophia* 1–3 presents at least two Marys, if not more, and employs multiple forms of this female name, including: (1) most often **ⲘⲀⲢⲒⲀ** ("Maria"; 175 times); (2) second in frequency: **ⲘⲀⲢⲒ2ⲀⲘ** ("Mariam"; 21 times); (3) followed lastly by **ⲘⲀⲢⲒ2ⲀⲘⲘⲎ** ("Mariamme"; occurring once, in *Pistis Sophia* 3.133). *Pistis Sophia* 1–3 helps to confirm Shoemaker's point that the form of Mary's name may not necessarily be reliable in determining which Mary is being discussed. In fact, in Jesus' dialogue with what appears to be the same figure named Mary, two different forms of her name appear in the same scene (see *Pistis Sophia* 1.19, 1.43, 3.108, and 3.128).

Determining the identity of this figure named Maria or Mariam is rather significant to these texts, as the number of references to the name are second in frequency only to the figure of Jesus himself. *Pistis Sophia* 1–3 contains approximately 197 references to these different Marys, which in

---

Pistis Sophia," *ZNW* 24 (1925): 218–40; idem, *Die Pistis Sophia, die beiden Bücher des Jeû, unbekanntes altgnostisches Werk* (ed. W. Till; vol. 1 of *Koptisch-gnostische Schriften;* 3d ed.; GCS 45; Berlin: Akademie-Verlag, 1954; repr., 1959, 1962). For more information, see also Michel Tardieu and Jean-Daniel Dubois, *Introduction à la littérature gnostique I* (Paris: Cerf and CNRS, 1986), 80–81.

[5] A lacuna of eight pages or four leaves exists at this point in the text.

the course of the text are sometimes differentiated from each other with the following additional designations: ⲘⲀⲢⲒⲀ ⲦⲘⲀⲀⲨ ("Mary the Mother")[6] and ⲘⲀⲢⲒⲀ ⲦⲘⲀⲄⲆⲀⲖⲎⲚⲎ ("Mary Magdalene"). These additional designations, however, are only minimally helpful in distinguishing the Marys from each other as there are only twelve explicit references to Mary Magdalene and only eleven to Mary the Mother.[7] Unfortunately, that leaves 174 references that do not specifically identify Mary as either the Mother or the Magdalene. I therefore understand Shoemaker's question concerning the validity of crediting Mary Magdalene with the bulk of the undesignated Marys in *Pistis Sophia*. Although it is reasonable to ask if Mary the Mother could instead be the primary figure to which the texts of *Pistis Sophia* refer, in the process of some intensive re-counting of references to these two figures, some interesting clues emerge that support Mary Magdalene as the primary figure.

2. Mary the Mother in Pistis Sophia 1–3

Let us begin by examining respectively the explicit identifications of Mary the Mother, first introduced into the text as ⲘⲘⲀⲢⲒⲀ ⲦⲀⲒ ⲈⲰⲀⲨⲘⲞⲨⲦⲈ ⲈⲢⲞⲤ ϪⲈ ⲦⲀⲘⲀⲀⲨ ⲔⲀⲦⲀ ⲠⲤⲰⲘⲀ ⲚⲐⲨⲖⲎ ("Mary, who is called my mother according to the material body" [*Pistis Sophia* 1.8]). The other explicit references to her in the text are ⲘⲀⲢⲒⲀ ⲦⲘⲀⲀⲨ ⲚⲒⲤ ("Maria the mother of Jesus Christ" [*Pistis Sophia* 1.59 twice, 1.61, and 1.62]), ⲘⲀⲢⲒⲀ ⲦⲈⲔⲘⲀⲀⲨ ("Maria your mother" [*Pistis Sophia* 1.62 twice]), and ⲘⲀⲢⲒⲀ ⲦⲈϥⲘⲀⲀⲨ ("Maria his mother" [*Pistis Sophia* 1.59, 1.61, and 1.62]). Following these references to Mary the Mother, the figure of Jesus responds to her several times with the words, "Excellent, well-done, Mary" (*Pistis Sophia* 1.59, 1.61, and 1.62). A critical evaluation, however, of this character's portrayal in the text as a whole reveals that these words, albeit nice praise, do not really set her apart from the rest of the group in any special way. The phrase, "Excellent, well-done," reflects instead the typical response Jesus makes to speakers throughout the volume, including, for example, Martha (*Pistis Sophia* 1.39), John (1.41), Thomas (2.70), Peter (2.65), James (2.68), and others as well.

---

[6] I continue the designation of this Mary as "the Mother" as opposed to "the Virgin" because such nomenclature reflects a later theological emphasis, and nowhere in *Pistis Sophia* is Mary the Mother designated as the Virgin. This epithet applies instead to "John the Virgin" (ⲒⲰϨⲀⲚⲚⲎⲤ ⲠⲠⲀⲢⲐⲈⲚⲞⲤ; *Pistis Sophia* 2.96) or the "Virgin of the Light" (ⲦⲠⲀⲢⲐⲈⲚⲞⲤ ⲘⲠⲞⲨⲞⲒⲚ; *Pistis Sophia* 1.59).

[7] The texts used for this essay will include quotes from the extant text presented by Carl Schmidt, ed., *Pistis Sophia* (trans. V. MacDermot; NHS 9; Leiden: Brill, 1978). The reference numbers are to the book followed by the chapter number.

Interestingly, all of the explicit references to Mary the Mother are confined to the first book of *Pistis Sophia*. Another intriguing aspect of these few occurrences of Mary the Mother are the references to her being part of the physical or material sphere, such as ΜΑΡΙΑ ΤΑΜΑΑΥ ΚΑΤΑ ΘΥΛΗ ΤΕΝΤΑΪϬΟΪΛΕ ("Maria my mother according to the matter to whom I was entrusted" [*Pistis Sophia* 1.61]). These words referring to her as "the matter to whom I was entrusted" echo Mary's introduction into the text as a "mother according to the material body" [*Pistis Sophia* 1.8]). The text reiterates again the concept of her being "entrusted" in the highest praise she receives from Jesus, "Truly, truly, I say that they will bless you from end to end of the earth for the pledge of the First Mystery was entrusted to you" (*Pistis Sophia* 1.59). It must be noted, however, that although the text acknowledges that others will bless her because of what was entrusted to her, Jesus does not. In a volume that philosophically tends to negate the physical realm, Mary the Mother's status does not appear to be an especially high one. Instead, her position is perhaps best encapsulated in Jesus' words to her, "From you has come forth the material body in which I exist, which I have cleaned and purified" (*Pistis Sophia* 1.59).[8]

3. Mary Magdalene As "the Other Mary"

Part of Shoemaker's argument that Mary the Mother must be the primary figure for this text rests upon the presence of an additional epithet, "the other Mary," for this second Mary who is not the Mother. He suggests that this phrase in all likelihood designates Mary Magdalene, thereby placing her in a secondary position in the text behind Mary the Mother. I agree that "the other Mary" may well be Mary Magdalene but disagree with his contention that: "Implicit in this distinction is the notion that the name Maria, if otherwise unadorned, signifies the Virgin, while any 'other Maria' must be specified as such."[9]

I suggest an alternative explanation—the use of this designation "the other Mary" for Mary Magdalene is not necessarily a description to place her in a subordinate position behind Mary the Mother but functions merely as a literary device to clarify and to transition back to the figure of Mary Magdalene after dialogue from Mary the Mother. This phrase occurs only twice in the text (*Pistis Sophia* 1.59 and 1.62), each time just after Mary the Mother has spoken, and does not appear to be implying a secondary

---

[8] Jesus commands the act of renunciation numerous times, including renouncing "the whole world and all the matter in it" (*Pistis Sophia* 2.95). Renunciation is a common theme for this text as a whole (see also 2.100 ["renounce the whole world and all its relationships"] as well as 3.102, 3.104, and 3.106).

[9] Shoemaker, "Mary and the Discourse of Orthodoxy," 185.

position for Mary Magdalene at all. In fact, when the term **ⲦⲔⲈⲘⲀⲢⲒ-
ⲀⲘ** ("the other Mary") is used, the text includes a significant additional
description—it refers to her as "the other Mary, the blessed one" (*Pistis
Sophia* 1.59):

> ⲘⲀⲢⲒⲀ ⲦⲘⲀⲀⲨ ⲚⲒⲤ ⲠⲈⲬⲀⲤ ... ⲒⲤ ⲠⲈⲬⲀϤ ⲬⲈ ⲚⲦⲞ Ⲟ̅ⲰⲰⲦⲈ ⲘⲀⲢⲒⲀ·
> ⲦⲀⲒ ⲈⲚⲦⲀⲤⲬⲒ-ⲘⲞⲢⲪⲎ ... ⲀⲨⲰ ⲀⲢⲈⲬⲒ-ⲈⲒⲚⲈ ... ⲚⲦⲞ ⲘⲚ̅ ⲦⲔⲈⲘⲀⲢⲒ-
> ⲀⲘ ⲦⲘⲀⲔⲀⲢⲒⲞⲤ·

> Mary the mother of Jesus said ... Jesus answered, "You also, Mary, you
> have received form ... and you have received likeness ... you and the
> other Mary, the blessed one." (*Pistis Sophia* 1.59)

I contend that these two descriptions used in conjunction with each other
for "the other Mary," that is, "the blessed one," provide us with an additional
hermeneutical key for unlocking the identity of some of the otherwise
undesignated Marys in the remainder of the text. The phrase "*the blessed
one*" (**ⲦⲘⲀⲔⲀⲢⲒⲀ**) in reference to Mary subsequently occurs numerous
times throughout the text and may, in fact, leave less ambiguity concerning
Mary's identity than previously thought. Through this particular passage
(*Pistis Sophia* 1.59) Mary "the blessed one" is clearly identified—as the *other*
one that is not the Mother—in all likelihood Mary Magdalene.[10]

4. Mary Magdalene in Pistis Sophia 1–3

The presence of this other character named Mary in *Pistis Sophia* 1–3
is clearly differentiated from Mary the Mother in twelve passages referring
to her as "Mary the Magdalene" (*Pistis Sophia* 2.83, 2.85, 2.87, 2.88, 2.90,
2.94, 2.96, 2.97, 2.98, 2.99, 3.127, 3.132).[11] These passages provide a different portrayal for this character than the one for Mary the Mother, as the

---

[10] I think one has to acknowledge the possibility of a third Mary in *Pistis Sophia*
1–3. The presence of a Martha in the text, for example, at least raises the possibility of the presence of Mary of Bethany. However, based on the absence of any
further designations or concrete indications of a third Mary, we will proceed with
Mary Magdalene as the most logical choice for "other Mary."

[11] It seems astonishing to me that a key figure of a text like Mary Magdalene
would be listed in the Schmidt/MacDermot index with only the first eight occurrences followed by an "etc." that supposedly covers the rest of the references (see
Schmidt, *Pistis Sophia,* 800). François Bovon makes a similar observation in his article, "Mary Magdalene's Paschal Privilege," in *New Testament Traditions and
Apocryphal Narratives* (trans. J. Haapiseva-Hunter; PTMS 36; Allison Park, Pa.: Pickwick, 1995), 232 n. 40. He points out that a significantly better index is available in
the German translation by Schmidt, *Pistis Sophia.*

following descriptions of Mary Magdalene indicate. For instance, the words following the text that **МАРІА ТМАГΔΑΛΗΝΗ** (Mary Magdalene) speaks relates that "the Savior marveled greatly at the answers to the words she gave" (*Pistis Sophia* 2.87). In the same passage Jesus then addresses Mary Magdalene as **ΤΕΠΝΕΥΜΑΤΙΚΗ ΝϨΙΛΙΚΡΙΝΕC** ("a pure spiritual one" [*Pistis Sophia* 2.87]). Mary Magdalene remains strong and intercedes on behalf of the others "who have despaired completely" (*Pistis Sophia* 2.94). The "power of light within Mary Magdalene welled up," and she offered an interpretation for Salome (*Pistis Sophia* 3.132). In response to one of Mary Magdalene's questions, Jesus says, "I will fulfill you in all powers and all pleromas ... so that you may be called the pleromas, fulfilled with all knowledge" (*Pistis Sophia* 2.85). Such encomiums for this Mary continue to add up throughout the text as the Savior announces in another passage that "Maria Magdalene [**МАРІА ТМАГΔΑΛΗΝΗ**] and John the Virgin [**ΙΩϨΑΝΝΗC ΠΠΑΡΘΕΝΟC**] will be superior to all my disciples" (*Pistis Sophia* 2.96).

When one compares the explicit references to Mary the Mother to those of Mary Magdalene, the references that bear especially high praise inevitably belong to Mary Magdalene. As these passages make clear, Jesus refers to **МАРІА ТМАГΔΑΛΗΝΗ** as "superior," as a "pure spiritual one," and even marvels at her answers. Thus the quality of these references swing the pendulum in favor of Mary Magdalene being the identity of the unspecified Mary and thus the primary interlocutor with Jesus in the text. Although this evidence alone concerning the explicit references to Mary has been sufficient for many scholars to perceive Mary Magdalene as the primary figure of the text, I offer below additional clues to help confirm such an interpretation by means of the following more subtle descriptions of Mary as "the other Mary," as the "blessed one," and as "the pure spiritual one."

5. Mary Magdalene As "the Blessed One"

The possibility that the epithet "the blessed one" refers to Mary Magdalene naturally calls for an examination of the other references to Mary "the blessed one." The first time that a Mary not referenced as the Mother appears in the text, she is addressed by Jesus with the following words:

> Jesus, the compassionate, answered and said to Mariam: "Mariam, the *blessed one* [**ТМАΚΑΡΙΑ**], whom I will complete in all the mysteries of the height, speak openly, you are she whose heart is more directed to the Kingdom of Heaven than all your brothers and sisters." (*Pistis Sophia* 1.17)

> Maria, the beautiful in her speech, came forward. The *blessed one* [**ТМАΚΑΡΙΑ**] prostrated herself. (*Pistis Sophia* 1.24)

> Now it happened when Jesus heard Mariam saying these words, he said
> to her: "Excellent, Mariam, *the blessed one* [ⲦⲘⲀⲔⲀⲢⲒⲀ], you pleroma or
> you all-blessed pleroma, who will be blessed among all generations."
> (*Pistis Sophia* 1.34)

Shoemaker suggests that such references be counted in favor of Mary the
Mother, as he contends that this epithet "would surely prompt an ancient
listener familiar with Luke's Gospel to associate this Mary with the Virgin
rather than the Magdalene."[12] These references are not, however, as he
suggests, "overlooked clues" that "interpreters failed to notice."[13] The
problem with his suggestion lies in the fact the epithet ⲦⲘⲀⲔⲀⲢⲒⲀ ("the
blessed one"—appearing at least seventeen times in the text either in the
feminine or masculine form) never appears in conjunction with explicit references to Mary the Mother. In fact, as we have just seen, the reference to
"the blessed one" explicitly refers to the Mary who is not the Mother (Jesus
spoke to his Mother, saying, "you and the other Mary, the blessed one"
[ⲚⲦⲞ ⲘⲚ ⲦⲔⲉⲘⲀⲢⲒⲈⲀⲘ ⲦⲘⲀⲔⲀⲢⲒⲞⲤ]; *Pistis Sophia* 1.59).

Nor is this passage the only instance of "the blessed one" not being
Mary the Mother. Another passage with its juxtaposition of speakers con-
firms the epithet of ⲦⲘⲀⲔⲀⲢⲒⲀ ("the blessed one") as a marker for the
Mary who is not the Mother:

> Jesus says, "Excellent, Mariam, *the blessed one* [ⲘⲀⲢⲒⲈⲀⲘ ⲦⲘⲀⲔⲀⲢⲒⲀ],
> who will inherit the whole Kingdom of the Light."

> After these things Mary, *the mother of Jesus* [ⲘⲀⲢⲒⲀ ⲦⲘⲀⲀⲨ ⲚⲒⲤ], also
> came forward and said: "My Lord and my Savior, command me also that
> I answer this discourse." (*Pistis Sophia* 1.61)

The subsequent text adds further praise for Mary, the blessed one (probably Mary Magdalene), as she is singled out again for a spiritual inheritance:
ⲉⲨⲄⲉ ⲘⲀⲢⲒⲈⲀⲘ ⲦⲈⲔⲖⲎⲢⲞⲚⲞⲘⲞⲤ ⲘⲠⲞⲨⲞⲉⲒⲚ ("Excellent, Mariam, you
inheritor of the light" [*Pistis Sophia* 1.62]). Given the way these examples
set this Mary apart from Mary the Mother, logically, then, the ensuing
occurrences of the phrase "Mary, the blessed one" should probably also be
counted as references to the Mary who is not the Mother.[14] The probability

---

[12] Shoemaker, "Mary and the Discourse of Orthodoxy," 186. See Luke 1:42 ("In
a loud voice she exclaimed: 'Blessed are you among women'") and 1:48 ("From
now on all generations will call me blessed").

[13] Shoemaker, "Mary and the Discourse of Orthodoxy," 186.

[14] In addition to Mary Magdalene, a few other disciples receive the term "the
blessed one" (ⲦⲘⲀⲔⲀⲢⲒⲀ [fem.]/ⲠⲘⲀⲔⲀⲢⲒⲞⲤ [masc.]). Philip is the first male disciple

increases that this description of Mary "the blessed one" (ⲦⲘⲀⲔⲀⲣⲓⲀ) refers to Mary Magdalene, for example, in this passage: "When the Savior heard these words that Maria [identified as Mary Magdalene in the preceding paragraph] spoke, he blessed her exceedingly" (*Pistis Sophia* 3.132).

Perhaps one of the underlying points of *Pistis Sophia* is that a disciple is called a "blessed one" for different reasons than being a Mother, as Shoemaker argues based on the first chapter of Luke. In fact, it is Luke who acknowledges the opposing point of view: "When a woman from the crowd said to Jesus, 'Blessed is the womb that gave you birth and the breasts that nursed you,' Jesus replied, 'Blessed rather are those who hear the word of God and keep it'" (Luke 11:27–28).

6. Mary Magdalene As "the Pure Spiritual One"

The text not only points toward Mary Magdalene as "the other one, the blessed one" but explicitly designates her with another epithet: ⲦⲉⲠⲛⲉⲨ-ⲘⲀⲦⲓⲔⲏ ⲚⲌⲓⲗⲓⲔⲣⲓⲛⲉⲥ ⲘⲀⲣⲓⲀ ("Maria, the pure spiritual one"). This phrase occurs for the first time in the section in which ⲘⲀⲣⲓⲀ ⲦⲘⲀⲅ-ⲆⲀⲗⲏⲛⲏ (Mary Magdalene) spoke and the Savior marveled greatly at her answers (*Pistis Sophia* 2.87). The text then reads: ⲉⲂⲟⲗ Ϫⲉ ⲛⲉⲀⲥⲣⲡⲛⲁ Ⲧⲏⲣⲥ ⲚⲌⲓⲗⲓⲔⲣⲓⲛⲉⲥ ("because she had completely become pure Spirit" [*Pistis Sophia* 2.87]). The Savior next praises her according to her spiritual state: ⲉⲨⲅⲉ ⲦⲉⲠⲛⲉⲨⲘⲀⲦⲓⲔⲏ ⲚⲌⲓⲗⲓⲔⲣⲓⲛⲉⲥ ⲘⲀⲣⲓⲀ ("Excellent, you pure spiritual one, Maria" [2.87]). In this case there is no doubt which Mary is being designated because the recipient of this praise is unquestionably Mary Magdalene, with additional references to Mary "the Magdalene" occurring shortly thereafter (in *Pistis Sophia* 2.88, 2.90, 2.94, 2.96, 2.97, 2.98, 2.99). Once this special designation of being "a pure spiritual one" appears at this site specifically referring to ⲘⲀⲣⲓⲀ ⲦⲘⲀⲅⲆⲀⲗⲏⲛⲏ, it occurs again in various forms in conjunction with the name Mary thereafter in 3.114, 3.116, 3.118, 3.120, 3.121, 3.122, and 3.130. It seems reasonable in these cases to judge these references as also referring to Mary Magdalene and not Mary the Mother. One would indeed be hard-pressed to attribute these references to Mary the Mother instead, since no explicit link

---

to speak (*Pistis Sophia* 1.22) and is given the special commission to record (1.43). He is subsequently identified as blessed (1.42 and 2.82), as are also Andrew (1.45), Thomas (2.70), Martha (2.80), and Peter (2.66) included in the plural ϨⲉⲛⲘⲀⲔⲀ-ⲣⲓⲟⲥ (1.37). John, interestingly, is called both: ⲠⲘⲀⲔⲀⲣⲓⲟⲥ ⲀⲨⲱ ⲠⲘⲉⲣⲓⲦ ("the blessed and beloved one" [2.90]). James does not receive the epithet ⲘⲀⲔⲀⲣⲓⲟⲥ but is twice referenced as ⲠⲘⲉⲣⲓⲦ (the "beloved" [2.68 and 2.78]). Lastly, none of the references clearly referring to Mary the Mother designates her as ⲦⲘⲀⲔⲀⲣⲓⲀ, as Mary Magdalene is.

between "a pure spiritual one" and Mary the Mother appears in this text, as it does with Mary Magdalene. Thus, these additional epithets and descriptions of Mary Magdalene reduce the contestability of her prominence and position both in the group and in the text of *Pistis Sophia* 1–3.[15]

7. Conclusion

I must admit in the end to having had some initial frustration with the text of *Pistis Sophia* 1–3 for not making the identity of the unspecified Mary clearer. I complained to myself that a text like this one with two Marys in it really could have been more helpful in its identifications and descriptions. After more intensive research, however, I have come to the conclusion that the text may not be as ambiguous as first meets the eye. In fact, the text offers numerous distinguishing, identifying phrases such as the "other one," "the blessed one," and the "pure spiritual one" to assist the reader in Mary's identification. I have shown that in each of these cases there is at least one if not more explicit links to Mary Magdalene with the result that Mary Magdalene's identity as the primary figure of *Pistis Sophia* 1–3 is difficult to dispute. If one takes into account not only the quality of the explicit identifications of Mary Magdalene in the text but also the abundant implicit descriptions and epithets, the primary status of Mary Magdalene in *Pistis Sophia* 1–3 is indeed the most persuasive and credible choice. In other words, the evidence on her behalf is definitely not as "inconclusive" as Shoemaker contends.

Ancient texts such as *Pistis Sophia* and the *Gospel of Mary* preserve literary representations of strong female figures who have not only heard the word but were also leaders in transmitting it. It is important to acknowledge that current debates concerning the identification of early Christian female leadership, especially the unspecified Mary, are more than merely scholarly exercises but have implications for recovering the authority of female leadership in the early church. This is especially relevant with respect to Mary Magdalene, whose apostolic example has proven pivotal in the debate concerning women's ordination in Christian congregations today.

---

[15] I would contend that in all probability Mary Magdalene is also the identity of the primary figure of Mary in *Pistis Sophia* 4 as well, but this case rests more on literary parallels and motifs than on textual grounds within the work itself and is beyond the scope of this article.

Why All the Controversy?
Mary in the *Gospel of Mary*

Karen L. King
Harvard University

1. Introduction

The last two centuries have seen the discovery of a variety of early Christian works (dating from the first or second[1] to the fourth centuries) in which Mary plays a prominent role among the disciples of Jesus in post-resurrection appearances.[2] Coupled with these discoveries has been an increased interest in the figure of Mary Magdalene in New Testament literature and Christian tradition more generally.[3] Consideration of the newly discovered works in the context of interest in Mary Magdalene has led to an increasingly widespread portrait of her as a purveyor or literary guarantor of a so-called "gnostic" Jesus tradition, as "the gnostic apostle."[4]

---

[1] The first- or second-century dating depends upon whether one dates the sayings in the *Gospel of Thomas* that mention Mary to the first or second century. Saying 114 is almost certainly a later second-century addition to the *Gospel of Thomas*.

[2] For a full list, see François Bovon, "Le privilège pascal de Marie-Madeleine," *NTS* 30 (1984): 50–62, translated as "Mary Magdalene's Paschal Privilege," in *New Testament Traditions and Apocryphal Narratives* (trans. J. Haapiseva-Hunter; PTMS 36; Allison Park, Pa.: Pickwick, 1995), 147–57; Antti Marjanen, *The Woman Jesus Loved: Mary Magdalene in the Nag Hammadi Library and Related Documents* (Nag Hammadi and Manichaean Studies 40; Leiden: Brill, 1996).

[3] See, for example, Susan Haskins, *Mary Magdalene: Myth and Metaphor* (New York: Harcourt Brace, 1993); Carla Ricci, *Mary Magdalene and Many Others: Women Who Followed Jesus* (trans. P. Burns; Minneapolis: Fortress, 1994); Jane Schaberg, "How Mary Magdalene Became a Whore," *BRev* 8, no. 5 (1992): 30–37, 51–52; Elisabeth Schüssler Fiorenza, *In Memory of Her: A Feminist Theological Reconstruction of Christian Origins* (New York: Crossroad, 1985); and idem, "Mary Magdalene: Apostle to the Apostles," *Union Theological Seminary Journal* (1975): 22–24.

[4] For example, in the first edition of the work, Till wrote: "Durch die überragende Rolle, die der Maria Magdalena am Schluß des ersten Teiles und im zweiten Teil des Evangeliums nach Maria zugeteilt wird, erscheint die bevorzugte Stellung

In this paper I would like to examine the portrait of Mary in one of the newly recovered texts, the *Gospel of Mary*.[5] Scholars are divided over the identity of Mary and her significance in this Gospel. First of all, which Mary is she: Mary Magdalene, Mary the virgin-mother, or some other Mary? And how important is Mary for the roles that are played by her character; that is, could some other disciple (male or female) be substituted without changing the meaning of the work? Or is the specific figure of Mary crucial to the interpretation of the *Gospel of Mary?* And if so, why? Is it because of a widespread tradition portraying her as a leading disciple or a visionary? What about her relation to "the Twelve"? Was the positive portrait of her and Levi[6] meant to counter a tradition that only the twelve male disciples were the true guarantors of apostolic tradition? Or is Mary the prime character because the work reflects historical reality, either that she was a leader in some segment of the early Christian movement or that she was designated the apostolic guarantor for some Christian tradition? Was that tradition gnostic? Was Mary a gnostic? If not, why might gnostics have chosen Mary as their guarantor? All of these questions regarding the figuration of Mary are related to the interpretation of inner-Christian controversies in the *Gospel of Mary* over such issues as the nature of discipleship and apostolic authority, the leadership roles of women, the meaning of Jesus' teachings, and the role of prophetic (visionary) experience in the formative centuries of Christianity.

First a quick look at the work itself. The *Gospel of Mary* survives in three manuscripts, two small third-century fragments in Greek, both from Oxyrhynchus,[7] and a more extensive copy in a fifth-century Coptic codex.[8]

---

der Maria Magdalene als Mittlerin und Verkünderin der gnostischen Lehre besonders betont. Hier wird sie ganz deutlich über die Apostel gestellt." See Walter C. Till and Hans-Martin Schenke, *Die gnostischen Schriften des koptischen Papyrus Berolinensis 8502* (2d ed.; TU 60; Berlin: Akademie-Verlag, 1972), 26. See also Robert M. Price, "Mary Magdalene: Gnostic Apostle?" *Grail* 6 (1990): 54–76.

[5] See Carl Schmidt, "Ein vorirenäisches gnostisches Originalwerk in koptischer Sprache," *SPAW.PH* 36 (1896): 839–47.

[6] Assuming here that Levi is not identified with Matthew.

[7] See P. J. Parsons, "3525: Gospel of Mary," in *The Oxyrhynchus Papyri* (London: Egypt Exploration Society, 1983), 50:12–14; C. H. Roberts, "463: The Gospel of Mary," in *Catalogue of the Greek Papyri in the John Rylands Library* (4 vols.; Manchester: Manchester University Press, 1911–52), 3:18–23; Dieter Lührmann, "Die griechischen Fragmente des Mariaevangeliums POxy 3525 und PRyl 463," *NovT* 30 (1988): 321–38.

[8] See Till and Schenke, *Die gnostischen Schriften;* Robert McL. Wilson and George MacRae, "The Gospel according to Mary," in *Nag Hammadi Codices V,2–5 and VI with Papyrus Berolinensis 8502,1 and 4* (ed. D. M. Parrott; NHS 11; Leiden: Brill, 1979), 453–71.

Because of the extremely fragmentary character of the Greek witnesses, our knowledge of the *Gospel of Mary* is heavily dependent upon the Coptic witness.

The first six pages are missing, so that the account begins in the midst of a dialogue between Jesus[9] and his disciples after the resurrection, followed by his admonition to go forth and preach the gospel of the kingdom (of the son of man/Child of Humanity).[10] He then departs. The missing introductory pages presumably held the standard elements of an appearance of Jesus to distressed disciples.[11] Thus we have what is generically a standard revelation dialogue framed as an appearance of the Savior to his disciples. What distinguishes the work, however, is the lengthy development of the disciples' response to the departure of the Savior before they actually depart to preach. Of the reckoned nineteen manuscript pages of the Coptic *Gospel of Mary,* approximately ten pages are taken up with the disciples' response to the Savior's commission and his departure. It is in this section of the work that scholars have perceived issues of inner-Christian controversy in the conflicts that erupt among the disciples. When the disciples are distraught at the Savior's departure, Mary steps in to comfort them, so that "she turned their heart [to]ward the Good, and they began to deba[t]e about the wor[d]s of [the Savior]."[12] Peter then points out that "the Savior loved you more than all other women," and he asks Mary to tell the other disciples "the words of the Savior that you remember." She agrees and proceeds to recount a lengthy dialogue with the Savior, unfortunately gapped by a five-page lacuna. When she finishes, Andrew states quite bluntly that he does not believe her words came from the Savior, "for indeed these teachings are strange." Peter goes further, questioning whether the Savior would have spoken "with a woman in private without our knowing about it. Are we to turn around and listen to her? Did he choose her over us?" Mary weeps, asking Peter if he really means to charge

---

[9] In the extant portions of the *Gospel of Mary,* this figure is not referred to by name ("Jesus") but as "Savior," "Blessed One," and "Lord."

[10] The Savior says: "Go then, preac[h] the good news about the kingdom" (4.8), but later in the text the disciples remember this injunction to regard "the gospel the kingdom of the son of man/the good news of the realm of the Child of Humanity" (5.2). All translations are my own. The numbering of the *Gospel of Mary* follows my translation in *The Complete Gospels* (ed. R. J. Miller; Sonoma, Calif.: Polebridge, 1992).

[11] See especially Judith Hartenstein, *Die zweite Lehre: Erscheinungen des Auferstandenen als Rahmenerzählung frühchristlicher Dialoge* (TU 146; Berlin: Akademie-Verlag, 2000), 128–29.

[12] All citations are from my own translation.

her with lying. Levi takes Mary's part, charging Peter with acting on the side of the adversaries who keep the soul imprisoned to the body and the passions. He affirms that the Savior "made her worthy," that the Savior's knowledge of her "is completely reliable," and that, yes indeed, "he did love her more than us." Levi exhorts the others to be ashamed of themselves and to do instead as the Savior commanded. Only now do they (or Levi)[13] go forth to teach and preach.

The literary conflicts among the apostles[14] have widely been read as reflecting historical controversies among second-century Christians.[15] Precisely what these issues are and what positions are taken by the *Gospel of Mary* are, however, still being determined. The remainder of this essay will review some of the major issues under debate and their significance for the literary figuration of Mary Magdalene in the *Gospel of Mary*.

2. Which Mary?

From the first publication of the Berlin manuscript by Till, the assumption has been that the Mary of the *Gospel of Mary* is the Mary from Magdala.[16] Arguments have been raised by Lucchesi[17] and Shoemaker[18]

---

[13] The Coptic (BG) says that "they" went out to preach and teach; the Greek fragment (PRyl.) says only that Levi began to announce the good news.

[14] I use the term "apostle" here (a term that does not appear in the work itself) only to refer to those who received the commission from the Savior to go forth and preach.

[15] This supposition is based not merely on the expression of conflict within the text's dialogue but on widespread external evidence from other sources that the issues raised here were widely under debate in this period. See, for example, Pheme Perkins, *The Gnostic Dialogue: The Early Church and the Crisis of Gnosticism* (Studies in Contemporary Biblical and Theological Problems; New York: Paulist, 1980), esp. 73.

[16] So Till and Schenke, *Die gnostische Schriften,* 26; Michel Tardieu, *Écrits gnostiques: Codex de Berlin* (Sources gnostiques et manichéennes 1; Paris: Cerf, 1984), 20; Anne Pasquier, *L'Évangile selon Marie* (BCNH.T 10; Québec: Les presses de l'Université Laval, 1983), 6; Karen L. King, "The Gospel of Mary Magdalene," in *A Feminist Commentary* (vol. 2 of *Searching the Scriptures;* ed. E. Schüssler Fiorenza; New York: Crossroad, 1994), 601; Marjanen, *The Woman Jesus Loved,* 94–95 n. 2.

[17] Enzo Lucchesi, "Évangile selon Marie ou Évangile selon Marie-Madeleine?" *AnBoll* 103 (1985): 366.

[18] Stephen J. Shoemaker, "Mary and the Discourse of Orthodoxy: Early Christian Identity and the Ancient Dormition Legends" (Ph.D. diss., Duke University, 1997), esp. ch. 4, "Mary in Early Christian Apocrypha: The Virgin's 'Gnostic' Past?" See Ann Graham Brock "Authority, Politics, and Gender in Early Christianity: Mary, Peter, and the Portrayal of Leadership" (Ph.D. diss., Harvard University, 2000).

that Mary might be the mother of Jesus. In his study of *The Woman Jesus Loved,* Antti Marjanen counters the arguments of Lucchesi, noting that the tradition that Jesus appeared also to his mother is relatively late (fourth century) and dependent upon the Johannine account (John 20:11–18). Similarly, the tradition that Mary the mother participates in dialogues of Jesus with the Twelve is sparsely attested compared to that of Mary Magdalene.[19] The recent Harvard dissertation of Ann Brock strengthens this argument by providing a systematic treatment of the figures of Peter and Mary Magdalene in a broad variety of early Christian literature.[20] She notes that they are often either alternatives in the appeal to apostolic authority or that they are set in conflict with each other. She further notes the processes whereby the virgin-mother takes over many of Mary Magdalene's roles. Silke Petersen's monograph on Mary Magdalene, Salome, and other women disciples of Jesus notes that the distinction between Mary Magdalene and the virgin-mother rests on gender presentation. The virgin-mother reinscribes the centrality of motherhood and women's subordination to men, while the depiction of Mary Magdalene consistently, albeit in various ways, contests gender definitions, for example, in promoting transcendence from sexuality and accompanying gender roles as the ideal.[21] This study, too, supports the identification of Mary with Mary Magdalene in the *Gospel of Mary.*

In the end, the value of asking the question has been to bring more attention precisely to the issue of the figuration of Mary Magdalene in the *Gospel of Mary.* It is her position as a known disciple of Jesus during his earthly mission, along with the apparently widespread tradition that she had received a vision/appearance of the risen Lord, that is the basis for her figuration in the *Gospel of Mary* as one of the apostles and as the recipient of a vision and special teaching. But while these features establish the traditional basis for the portrayal, they do not yet explain the thematization of conflict in the work. Silke Petersen's work, however, offers an insight. She concluded from her study of Mary Magdalene in "gnostic Christianity" that:

> The conflict around Mary Magdalene in Gnostic writings is bound up with two themes: her being a woman and her special relationship to Jesus.... In almost all Gnostic writings in which Mary appears, a controversy over

---

[19] See Marjanen, *The Woman Jesus Loved,* 94–95 n. 2.

[20] See Brock, "Authority, Politics, and Gender."

[21] See Silke Petersen, *"Zerstört die Werke der Weiblichkeit!" Maria Magdalena, Salome und andere Jüngerinnen Jesu in christlich-gnostischen Schriften* (Nag Hammadi and Manichaean Studies 48; Leiden: Brill, 1999), 303–4.

the significance of womanhood or femininity simultaneously is engaged. Herein lies the most significant difference to the New Testament writings, as well as to later writings of non-Gnostic provenance.[22]

If we were, therefore, to ask what difference it makes that the role of the leading disciple in *Gospel of Mary* is played by Mary Magdalene and not some other (male) disciple, the answer is that it allows for the thematization of women's roles and gender, notably in ways that contest normative gender definitions or women's social subordination.

How does the figuration of Mary function to thematize these issues?

3. Mary As a Woman

It is because Mary Magdalene is a woman apostle that the question of gender in leadership roles can be thematized in the *Gospel of Mary*. As I have argued elsewhere,[23] the work does this explicitly through the figuration of conflict with Peter. He asks Mary to speak to the other disciples because, as he tells her, "We know that the Savior loved you more than all other women." After she finishes speaking, he instead challenges: "Did (the Savior) choose her over us?" It would seem he got more than he bargained for in Mary's teaching. In the Berlin Codex, she says that she will tell the other disciples "what has been hidden from you" (ⲡⲉⲑⲏⲡ ⲉⲣⲱⲧⲛ̄; BG 8502, 10.8); in the Oxyrhynchus papyrus she says only that she will tell them what she remembers that is unknown to them (ὅσα ὑμᾶς λανθάνει καὶ ἀπομνημονεύω; P.Oxy. 3525, line 18). Either way, her dialogue with the Savior illustrates that he gave her teaching more advanced than that given to the other disciples. Peter's refusal to accept Mary's teaching is an acknowledgment of this spiritual advantage, as well as an expression of his jealousy. Levi points out to Peter that the Savior's judgment is reliable and that he did indeed love Mary more than the others. It is on the basis of this relationship to the Savior that her authority to teach rests.

---

[22] Ibid., 104: "Der Streit um Maria Magdalena ist in den gnostischen Schriften mit zwei Themen verbunden: Ihrem Frau-Sein und ihrer besonderen Beziehung zu Jesus.... In fast allen gnostischen Schriften, in denen Maria auftritt, begegnet damit gleichzeitig eine Auseinandersetzung mit der Bedeutung des Frau-Seins und der Weiblichkeit. Hierin liegt der deutlichste Unterschied sowohl zu den neutestamentlichen Texten wie auch zu den späteren Schriften nichtgnostischer Provenienz."

[23] See King, "The Gospel of Mary Magdalene," and "Prophetic Power and Women's Authority: The Case of the Gospel of Mary Magdalene," in *Women Preachers and Prophets through Two Millennia of Christianity* (ed. B. M. Kienzle and P. J. Walker; Berkeley and Los Angeles: University of California Press, 1998), 21–41.

That the Savior chose well is illustrated by the fact that she alone (apparently) is not distraught and does not fear when the Savior leaves. She is able to calm and comfort the other disciples and turn their thoughts toward the Good and to a discussion of the words of the Savior. After she sees the vision, the Lord praises her for her stability of character and mind. It is clear that she steps into the role of the Savior at his departure, teaching and exhorting the disciples. She exercises leadership not based on any office but as a response to their need and because she possesses the spiritual qualities necessary to the task. In short, the *Gospel of Mary* presents her as an exemplary disciple-apostle, and a leader even of male disciples. The conflict between Mary and Peter thematizes the issue of women's roles quite directly.

Why this support of women's leadership? Pheme Perkins writes that she is:

> skeptical of those who use this picture of Mary to claim that Gnostics upheld community leadership by women in opposition to the male dominated hierarchy of the orthodox Church; . . . Mary is the hero here not because of an extraordinary role played by women in Gnostic communities, but because she is a figure closely associated with Jesus to whom esoteric tradition may be attached. Gnostic writings share a common presupposition of ancient ascetic writings: "Femininity is to be destroyed."[24]

Perkins helpfully points out here that the mere fact of a woman in a position of leadership does not necessarily reflect a positive valuation of women. Antti Marjanen's analysis of the figure of Mary in Nag Hammadi and related literature illustrates this point well. He concludes that "It is conspicuous that despite the prominent role the Gnostic writings grant to Mary Magdalene many of them can use a language which devalues women."[25] Indeed, study of Nag Hammadi and heresiological literature illustrates a wide variety of uses of gender imagery for various purposes.[26] In general, however, three models prevail: (1) the ideal (often the transcendent or noetic) is gendered as masculine; the lower (often the material or passionate nature) is gendered as female; (2) the ideal is figured as male-female (androgynous); the "fallen" condition is the division into male and female; and (3) the ideal is nongendered; gender and sexuality belong to the lower sphere. There is no correlation between these

---

[24] Perkins, *Gnostic Dialogue,* 136 n. 10.

[25] Marjanen, *The Woman Jesus Loved,* 220.

[26] See, for example, Karen L. King, ed., *Images of the Feminine in Gnosticism* (SAC; Philadelphia: Fortress, 1988; repr., Philadelphia: Trinity Press International, 2000).

models and specific social practices. For example, one can find texts that employ the first model symbolically to associate materiality with the feminine in order to advocate sexual asceticism,[27] to promote the ideal of women as mothers,[28] or to model spiritual perfection as transformation (from female to male).[29] It is therefore necessary to ask in each instance both what model of gender is being deployed and to what ends.[30] The *Gospel of Mary* deploys model 3, but to what ends? The *Gospel of Mary* affirms that men and women exercise leadership on the basis of spiritual maturity, not on gender or sexual identity.

In *The Gnostic Gospels,* Elaine Pagels suggested that Christian groups that accepted female as well as male imagery for God were more likely to accept women's leadership roles within their communities.[31] While Pagels's correlation of female divine imagery and women's increased status is generally accurate,[32] the *Gospel of Mary* does not use feminine imagery for the divine. The divine is figured only in neutral terms as "the Good." Here the gender model is number 3 above: the divine, transcendent sphere is non-gendered, while sex and gender belong to the lower sphere. The theological basis for this position lies in the *Gospel of Mary*'s understanding that the true self is not the body, but spiritual even as the divine is nonmaterial and spiritual. The advocacy of women's leadership is therefore not tied to figuring the divine as feminine[33] but rather to the irrelevance of bodily nature for spiritual authority. Rejection of the body as the self implied that the gender roles based on sex were not a part of one's true spiritual identity. Unlike Tertullian, who thought that souls themselves were material and had sex-gender, the *Gospel of Mary* sees the soul as nonmaterial, transcending sexual differences.

---

[27] For example, *The Book of Thomas the Contender.*

[28] For example, 1 Timothy.

[29] For example, *Gospel of Thomas* 114.

[30] Some texts will use more than one model of gender, complicating the analysis.

[31] See Elaine Pagels, *The Gnostic Gospels* (New York: Random House, 1981), 48–69, esp. p. 66.

[32] See, for example, Karen L. King, *Women and Goddess Traditions in Antiquity and Today* (SAC; Minneapolis: Fortress, 1997). The cross-cultural essays in this volume were designed to ask precisely this question: Are goddesses good for women in terms of raising their social status and general well-being?

[33] Although the *Gospel of Mary* never uses feminine metaphors or grammatically feminine terms for the Divine, at the same time the text does not use strongly masculine imagery for God either. The Divine is called "the Good," and the soul's final attainment is described spatially as ascent and more generally as a release from time, from forgetfulness, and from sound.

This perspective potentially implied two things for women. First, a woman's identity and spirituality could be developed apart from her roles as wife and mother or slave,[34] whether she actually withdrew from those roles or not. Second, she could exercise leadership on the basis of spiritual achievement apart from the low status accorded to her as woman in society at large. The rejection of the body as the self opened up the possibility of an ungendered space within the Christian community in which leadership functions were based on spiritual achievement, illustrated by prophetic inspiration and stability of character.[35] Peter's fault lay in his inability to see beyond the body to the spiritual character of a person. His contention of Mary's leadership illustrates his unstable[36] character and lack of spiritual maturity. It illustrates, too, that those who opposed this kind of women's leadership did so out of false pride, jealousy, lack of understanding, spiritual immaturity, and contentiousness.

Mary as a woman is therefore crucial to the thematization of women's roles, but her sex-gender is also crucial to emphasizing the *theological* teaching of the *Gospel of Mary* concerning the body and salvation. For the *Gospel of Mary,* the body is not the true self. Even as God is nongendered, immaterial, and transcendent, so too is the true human self.[37] The Savior tells his disciples that they get sick and die "because you love what deceives you" (*Gos. Mary* 3.7–8). Peter sees only that Mary is a woman (her bodily nature), not that she is a spiritually mature disciple. He apparently "loves" the status his male sex-gender gives him, and that leads to pride and jealousy. Levi's correction of Peter's charge helps the reader to see one of the primary ways in which people are deceived by the body. This insight is effective only because Mary was a woman.

4. Mary As an Apostle

The choice of her as the main protagonist in the *Gospel of Mary* carries other implications as well, beyond her being a woman. The first is

---

[34] I mention slave women here because the assumption in antiquity was that a woman's sexuality belonged to her master. Hence slave women were often seen as sexually polluted as a matter of status. The kind of Christian community idealized by the *Gospel of Mary* could potentially offer slave women the opportunity to cultivate a social identity in which their sexuality was not a defining factor.

[35] This position is developed in King, "Prophetic Power and Women's Authority."

[36] For the importance of the theme of stability as an indication of spiritual maturity, see Michael Allen Williams, *The Immovable Race: A Gnostic Designation and the Theme of Stability in Late Antiquity* (NHS 29; Leiden: Brill, 1985).

[37] In the *Gospel of Mary,* this self is referred to as "the child of humanity" or "the perfect Human."

the question of her figuration as an apostle. Was she or wasn't she? Early studies[38] assumed that Mary was not an apostle, due to hegemonic notions associating apostleship with men only, especially the Twelve.

Helmut Koester has shown that the limitation of the appellation "apostle" to a limited group of male disciples (especially the Twelve) is only one way in which the term was used in the first two centuries of Christianity.[39] Bernadette Brooten, for example, has demonstrated that Paul used the term "apostle" of a woman, Junia, in Rom 16:7,[40] and Ann Brock's recent study of apostolic authority further supports the view that apostolic authority was not limited to the Twelve in early tradition.[41]

I have argued that Mary is regarded as one of the Savior's disciples throughout the work, not merely in the second half.[42] Her role in the text presumes that she was regarded by readers as an apostle, as one of those who received the Savior's commission to go forth and preach the gospel.[43]

---

[38] In the first edition of the Berlin Codex, Walter Till argued that Mary plays the main role in the second half of the work, where her teaching is the main topic, but that she played little or no role in the first part of the work, the Savior's appearance and dialogue with his disciples. Indeed, he suggested that these two parts were originally independent works and that the scene where Mary comforts the distraught disciples at the end of part one was added to link the two otherwise completely unrelated works (see Till and Schenke, *Die gnostischen Schriften,* 26). Till clearly does not count Mary as one of the apostles but states rather that the *Gospel of Mary* "elevates her over the apostles." Till of course published this work before knowing the Nag Hammadi texts in which Mary is reckoned among the disciples/apostles in a variety of works classified as revelation dialogues (such as *Dialogue of the Savior, Sophia of Jesus Christ, First Apocalypse of James*), but he does note the corresponding portrait of Mary in *Pistis Sophia*. Nonetheless, he does not treat Mary as an apostle. Pheme Perkins classifies the Mary of the *Gospel of Mary* among "the non-apostles" (the chapter title is "Those Whom Jesus Loves: The Non-apostles"). She wrongly translates *Gos. Mary* 18.10–16, saying that Mary "is called 'the one whom the Savior loved more than the apostles because of her gnosis' (18, 10–16)." She then concludes: "She clearly represented the Gnostic claim to a truth greater than that contained in the apostolic tradition" (*Gnostic Dialogue,* 134).

[39] See Helmut Koester, "La tradition apostolique et les origines du Gnosticisme," *RTP* 119 (1987): 1–16.

[40] See Bernadette Brooten, "'Junia ... Outstanding among the Apostles' (Romans 16:7)," in *Women Priests: A Catholic Commentary on the Vatican Declaration* (ed. L. Swidler and A. Swidler; New York: Paulist, 1977), 141–44.

[41] See Brock, "Authority, Politics, and Gender," esp. 1–40, 212–14.

[42] As Till contended in Till and Schenke, *Die gnostischen Schriften,* 26 (see also King, "The Gospel of Mary Magdalene," 610).

[43] So, too, in *Sophia of Jesus Christ* the Savior commissions his disciples (twelve men and seven women), and at the end of the work they begin to preach the gospel.

It would seem that the *Gospel of Mary* reflects a time and place at which the exclusive tradition of the Twelve was not fixed. Indeed, our concerns about whether women were numbered among the apostles, tied as it is to contemporary arguments for or against women's ordination, was simply not a concern to the *Gospel of Mary* at all.

The controversy between Mary and Levi, on the one hand, and Peter and Andrew on the other, is not about who is an apostle—indeed the term is never used—but about who has understood and appropriated the teachings of the Savior. The question at issue is who is able to preach the gospel. The *Gospel of Mary* is quite clear that having followed Jesus or encountered the risen Lord and received teaching and commission from him is not sufficient. All the disciples receive teaching and commission, but only Mary is figured as a model disciple. Only Levi defends her. By portraying the other disciples, especially Andrew and Peter, as disturbed and uncomprehending even after the resurrection and by contrasting them with the steadfastness of Mary, the *Gospel of Mary* clearly questions apostolic witness as a sufficient basis for preaching the gospel. Why?

5. Disciples in Conflict

What is the significance of portraying the disciples in conflict after the resurrection? Earlier Gospels, notably the Gospel of Mark, had portrayed the disciples as vying for prominence with each other or as not fully understanding Jesus' teaching. In the Gospel of Mark, these occasions serve to provide an opportunity for Jesus to clarify to the reader what is the correct understanding of his teaching, his death, or his vision for community and leadership. In the *Gospel of Mary,* however, this conflict and misunderstanding take place after the resurrection. Here, too, the conflict allows for the text to correct wrong thinking and to elaborate on its own theological perspectives.

What are those perspectives? Three suggestions have been made: (1) that the portrayal contrasts prophetic-visionary experience with mere apostolic succession in order to affirm the first as a more sure sign of legitimate authority; (2) that the portrayal affirms the gnostic teacher (especially Mary) against the representatives of orthodoxy (Andrew and especially Peter); and (3) that the portrayal contrasts the Twelve (represented by Andrew and Peter) with other spiritually advanced disciples (Mary and Levi) in order to undermine claims to exclusive (male) authority. Let's consider each of these suggestions.

5.1. Visions or Succession?

Pagels has already made the point that the controversy among the disciples reflects the tension between later priests and bishops who claimed authority based on seeing themselves as the successors of the immediate followers of Jesus—represented in the text by Peter and Andrew—and those who thought authority should be based on spiritual gifts, especially prophetic experience—represented by Mary Magdalene.[44] Indeed "Gnostics," she says, "recognized three sources of revelation apart from the common tradition mediated through the apostles": from secret apostolic tradition, from visions, and from within oneself, through direct spiritual experience and inspiration.[45] All three apply to the figuration of Mary in the *Gospel of Mary*.[46]

In my own work, I too have assumed that Mary's vision took place after the resurrection, putting its contents in competition with transmission of the public ministry.[47] I had assumed that the account of her vision began with the statement, "I saw the Lord in a vision, and I said to him, 'Lord, today I saw you in a vision,'" and continued through Mary's account of the final rise of the soul to rest (e.g., *Gos. Mary* 7–9). Judith Hartenstein argues, however, that Mary is reporting on a vision she had during the ministry of the historical Jesus and a conversation with him later the same day about the vision. In this case, she argues, the *Gospel of Mary* is "no reference for continuing revelation through visions."[48] Instead she insists that

---

[44] See Pagels, *Gnostic Gospels,* 13–14.

[45] Elaine Pagels, "Visions, Appearances, and Apostolic Authority: Gnostic and Orthodox Traditions," in *Gnosis: Festschrift für Hans Jonas* (ed. B. Aland; Göttingen: Vandenhoeck & Ruprecht, 1978), 426–27. Andrew and Peter, Pagels notes, look "to past events, suspicious of those who 'see the Lord' in vision," while Mary "claims to experience his continuing presence" (*Gnostic Gospels,* 13–14). Pagels has further argued that: "From these [gnostic] accounts we observe, *first,* that the authority and commission of the disciples (or 'apostles') depends not on the witness to the resurrection for which ecclesiastical Christians revere them, but on special visions and revelations that go beyond orthodox tradition. *Second,* the accounts define that authoritative circle in different ways.... Despite their differences these texts [*Apocalypse of Paul, Letter of Peter to Philip, Dialogue of the Savior*] seem to agree—against ecclesiastical tradition—that belonging to the original circle of disciples (or 'apostles') matters less than receiving new and continuing visions" ("Visions, Appearances," 422). For Pagels, the *Gospel of Mary* represents the most extreme of these works insofar as "the disciples consent to receive this revelation from Mary, acknowledging that her direct contact with the Lord through visions surpasses their own" ("Visions, Appearances," 425).

[46] This position regarding the sources of revelation, she argues, correlates with a "devaluation of the apostles' original witness," and resulted in a strong response from ecclesiastical Christianity in legitimizing "a hierarchy of persons through whose authority in teaching and discipline all others must approach God" (Pagels, "Visions, Appearances," 425, 430).

[47] See King, especially "Prophetic Power and Women's Authority."

[48] Hartenstein, *Die zweite Lehre,* 130; see also n. 14, contra Pagels, Pasquier, King, and Marjanen; in n. 141 on p. 153, she adds a reference to Petersen.

the topic of the vision was brought up only as a starting point for the discussion of how visions take place. This point is confirmed, she continues, by the fact that Peter only objects that Mary received teaching in private, not that she received it through visions.[49]

I think this is wonderfully insightful. It solves the problem of Mary's use of the perfect tense with the present ("I *saw* you in a vision *today*") and the oddness of discussing the visionary experience within the vision.[50] It still leaves the problem of the oddity of having a vision of Jesus and then seeing the earthly Jesus later on the same day, but here Hartenstein points to the transfiguration in Matt 17:1–13, and one might also consider the recently published *Gospel of the Savior,* where it may be that both the Savior and the disciples experience an ascent before the crucifixion.[51] If Mary's vision took place during the preresurrection ministry of Jesus, it could imply that she saw him as he truly was in all his glory, that is, that she understood his true divine nature already during his public ministry.[52] That would also make sense of the Savior's response to Mary: "Blessed are you for not wavering at the sight of me" (*Gos. Mary* 7.3). At any rate, as Hartenstein points out, Mary's vision and her stability point toward her worthiness to receive special teaching from Jesus.[53] In the end, Hartenstein's point is that the contrast in the portrayal of the disciples' worthiness as apostles (e.g., Peter versus Mary) in the *Gospel of Mary* is not based on whether their teaching relies upon the historical Jesus or upon continuing visions.

5.2. Gnostic versus Orthodox

Instead, Hartenstein understands the contrasting portrayal of the disciples in terms of orthodox versus gnostic teaching. Here Peter and Andrew represent orthodoxy; Mary and Levi, Gnosticism. According to the *Gospel of Mary*'s perspective, those who teach a gnostic understanding of the Savior's teaching are the true apostles.

We can begin this discussion by asking: Was Mary Magdalene a gnostic? The answer to this question is no, if we mean that the historical Mary Magdalene held the views delimited by modern scholars, for example, Hans Jonas's famous essay on "The Delimitation of the Gnostic Phenomenon." If

---

[49] Ibid., 153.

[50] See King, "Prophetic Power and Women's Authority," 24.

[51] See Charles W. Hedrick and Paul A. Mirecki, *Gospel of the Savior: A New Ancient Gospel* (Santa Rosa, Calif.: Polebridge, 1999).

[52] Perkins already made this point in passing, in comparison with the *Apocalypse of Peter;* see *Gnostic Dialogue,* 133.

[53] Hartenstein, *Die zweite Lehre,* 154.

one means by this question that the views ascribed to Mary Magdalene in the *Gospel of Mary* are gnostic, then the answer is yes or no, depending upon how one defines "Gnosticism." This latter question has focused primarily on two issues: (1) Does the *Gospel of Mary* presuppose a "gnostic myth" through its presentation of "typical gnostic themes"? (2) Does the genre of the *Gospel of Mary* belong to Gnosticism? I want to take up the question of genre first.

Genre. The *Gospel of Mary* has been categorized as a "gnostic revelation dialogue"[54] or "discourse."[55] According to Pheme Perkins, "the revelation dialogue seems to have been as characteristic of Christian Gnostics as the Gospel was of orthodox Christians."[56] Here she is following the line of argument suggested by James Robinson[57] and Helmut Koester that certain distinct genres of early Christian literature developed to express distinct christological tendencies.[58] The narrative Gospel was always based on the kerygma of the crucified and risen Lord; the sayings Gospel, on the other hand, as exemplified by the *Gospel of Thomas,* was catalyzed as a genre by "the view that the kingdom is uniquely present in Jesus' eschatological preaching and that eternal wisdom about man's true self is disclosed in his words. The gnostic proclivity of this concept needs no further elaboration."[59] Furthermore, according to Koester, the features of the framework of the revelation discourse, such as one sees in the *Apocryphon of John*'s account of a luminous appearance to the disciple John, "cannot be derived from the resurrection appearances of the canonical gospels, even though a number of gnostic revelations admittedly have been influenced by the canonical Easter stories."[60]

---

[54] See, for example, Perkins, *Gnostic Dialogue.*

[55] Henri-Charles Puech and Beate Blatz, "The Gospel of Mary," in *Gospels and Related Writings* (vol. 1 of *New Testament Apocrypha;* ed. W. Schneemelcher; trans. R. McL. Wilson; rev. ed.; Cambridge: Clarke; Louisville: Westminster John Knox, 1991), 391.

[56] Perkins, *Gnostic Dialogue,* 26.

[57] Perkins cites Robinson, "On the Gattung of Mark (and John)," in *Gnostic Dialogue,* 26 n. 3.

[58] See Koester in James M. Robinson and Helmut Koester, *Trajectories through Early Christianity* (Philadelphia: Fortress, 1971), 158–204.

[59] Koester in Robinson and Koester, *Trajectories,* 186.

[60] Ibid., 195. In his foundational work, *Ancient Christian Gospels: Their History and Development* (Philadelphia: Trinity Press International; London: SCM, 1990), Helmut Koester presents the development of his thesis that sayings collections and dialogue Gospels generally precede literarily narrative Gospels.

While accepting the existence of the dialogue genre, two studies have recently criticized this general theory regarding the relationship between genre and Christology. Martina Janßen has noted the wide diversity of content, form, and function of dialogues in ancient literature, and argued that the evidence does not support tying a "gnostic" theological content to this genre.[61] On the contrary, she suggests that the so-called "gnostic revelation dialogue" is an artificial construct that distorts interpretation, especially by oversimplification of the diversity among the texts so classified. In short, she problematizes the connection between dialogue form and "gnostic" theological content.

Judith Hartenstein takes a different tack by examining the frame narratives of the revelation dialogues, isolating a subtype of appearance dialogue. She concludes that it is the frame narrative relating an appearance of Jesus to his disciples after the resurrection that consistently marks a clear Christian element in these texts and provides a clear connection to the New Testament gospels. In short, she argues that such appearance frameworks show a dependence upon the narrative Gospels,[62] while the content of the dialogues can be quite diverse both in origin and content.[63] It is, in short, precisely the genre of the work that gives it its Christian (as opposed to gnostic) character, although in the end Hartenstein supports the view that the *Gospel of Mary* is a gnostic work, that is, not because of the genre, but because of the content of Jesus and Mary's teachings.

Is the Gospel of Mary *Gnostic?* From the first publication of the *Gospel of Mary*, its gnostic character was assumed.[64] Indeed, one scholar went so far as to suggest that the work was not even Christian.[65] Some scholars early on argued that the controversy in the *Gospel of Mary* represented a historical situation of conflict between gnostic and orthodox Christians. Perkins, for example, suggested that Mary represents the gnostic position, while

---

[61] See Martina Janßen, "Mystagogus Gnosticus? Zur Gattung der 'gnostischen Gespräche des Auferstandenen,'" in *Studien zur Gnosis* (ed. G. Lüdemann; Arbeiten zur Religion und Geschichte des Urchristentums 9; Frankfurt am Main: Lang, 1999), 21–260.

[62] Here Hartenstein abandons her methodology of intertextuality for the usual methods of literary dependency and source criticism.

[63] The content of the dialogues is not subjected to analysis in Hartenstein's work, but only the frame narratives.

[64] See Till and Schenke, *Die gnostischen Schriften,* 26–32.

[65] See Robert McL. Wilson, "The New Testament in the Gnostic Gospel of Mary," *NTS* 3 (1956–57): 236–43.

Peter represents the orthodox.[66] This view continues to be quite alive in studies of the work, and most studies have presupposed that a gnostic myth[67] or typical gnostic themes[68] lie behind the work.

One way scholars have supported this position is by comparing the teaching of the *Gospel of Mary* with standard interpretations of the New Testament, thereby anachronistically setting up a contemporary under-standing of orthodox Christianity against which the *Gospel of Mary* fails. It being assumed already, then, that the *Gospel of Mary* is heretical, it only remains to ask what kind of heresy. Contemporary scholars have tended to divide the earliest forms of Christianity into two types: Jewish Christian-ity and Gnosticism. Jewish Christianity is characterized by too much or too positive an appropriation of "Judaism."[69] Gnosticism is characterized by too little or too negative an appropriation of "Judaism." Orthodoxy is just right, rejecting "Jewish error" but correctly (from the orthodox perspective) claiming the heritage of Scripture for its own.

Attempts by scholars to characterize the essential features of Gnosti-cism, such as we see, for example, in the now-classic work of Hans Jonas,[70] are less self-evident than they used to be, given the variety of the literature from the Nag Hammadi discoveries.[71] Already in 1961, Carsten Colpe had shown that "the gnostic redeemer myth" was itself an artificial

---

[66] Perkins, *Gnostic Dialogue,* 136, 141. She suggested that "the picture of Mary in *Gospel of Mary* was formulated in association with a Gnostic sayings tradition" (135).

[67] See, for example, Pasquier, *L'Évangile selon Marie,* 5–7; Hartenstein, *Die zweite Lehre,* 137.

[68] Petersen, *"Zerstört die Werke der Weiblichkeit!"* 60–61. She determines the *Gospel of Mary* to have non-Christian, gnostic content primarily by: (1) marking out "typical Gnostic themes" (e.g., the rise of the soul as release from matter; the con-trast between the inner and the outer, so that peace and salvation comes from within a person and not from without; the Son of Man is not the judge of the end-time, but the true Human in humanity); and (2) comparison with the New Testament.

[69] I put the term *Judaism* in quote marks here to signal an acknowledgment of the gap between the Christian construction of "Judaism" and a historical descrip-tion of Jewish beliefs and practices.

[70] Hans Jonas, "Delimitation of the Gnostic Phenomenon—Typological and His-torical," in *Le origini dello Gnosticismo* (ed. U. Bianchi; SHR 12; Leiden: Brill, 1967), 90–108; idem, *Die mythologische Gnosis* (vol. 1 of *Gnosis und spätantiker Geist;* 3d ed.; Göttingen: Vandenhoeck & Ruprecht, 1964); idem, *The Gnostic Religion: The Message of the Alien God and the Beginnings of Christianity* (2d ed.; Boston: Bea-con, 1958).

[71] See, for example, Michael Allen Williams, *Rethinking "Gnosticism": An Argu-ment for Dismantling a Dubious Category* (Princeton, N.J.: Princeton University Press, 1996).

and inaccurate scholarly construction.[72] More recently, Michael Williams has demonstrated the inadequacy of typological definitions of Gnosticism to characterize accurately the variety of materials grouped under this rubric.[73] It is increasingly apparent that the reification of the (normative) rhetorical category of Gnosticism into a monolithic historical entity is untenable. The bifurcating frame of orthodoxy and heresy (here represented as orthodoxy versus Gnosticism) does not do justice to the theological or sociological diversity of early Christianity. Appeal to a "gnostic redeemer myth" or "typical gnostic themes" is no longer sufficient to determine the social or theological setting of a work like the *Gospel of Mary*.

Some themes in the *Gospel of Mary* that have been identified as "gnostic," such as the rise of the soul as release from matter or the distinction between inner and outer, are commonplaces of ancient philosophy. Nor are the most distinctive themes of Gnosticism, such as the distinction between a lower demiurgic creator (modeled on the God of Genesis) and a higher transcendent Deity, present in the *Gospel of Mary*. The rise of the soul as release from matter, salvation as an inner process of turning toward God, or a Christology that either rejects or simply does include the notion of Christ as judge—these are all ideas that early Christians experimented with in their theology making. That they did not make it vis-à-vis later determinations of orthodoxy does not mean either that they were regarded as non-Christian in their own day. Rather, the conflict between the disciples in the *Gospel of Mary* shows all the markers of inner-Christian conflict in which Christians with different views cannot yet appeal to fixed norms, either orthodox or heretical.

What is important for my argument here is not whether Gnosticism ever existed or not, but whether the conflict among the apostles in the *Gospel of Mary* can be characterized as an intentional conflict of orthodox versus gnostic disciples. The answer to that question is no. In framing the problem this way, we miss the historical significance of the work's own rhetoric of conflict and the complex dynamics of early Christian social and theological formation.

5.3. Twelve against All Comers

A third option for understanding the conflicting figurations of the disciples is to see it as a rhetoric of the Twelve (represented again by Peter and Andrew) against all comers (represented by Mary and Levi). Hartenstein

---

[72] See Carsten Colpe, *Die religionsgeschichtliche Schule: Darstellung und Kritik ihres Bildes vom gnostischen Erlösermythus* (FRLANT NS 60; Göttingen: Vandenhoeck & Ruprecht, 1961).

[73] See Williams, *Rethinking Gnosticism*.

notes, again perceptively, that this choice of figures pits two of the Twelve (Peter and Andrew) over against two not of the Twelve (Mary and Levi, arguing that Levi is not identified with Matthew at this stage of tradition).[74] That might indicate that the *Gospel of Mary* is consciously polemicizing against the Twelve.

On the other hand, she argues that the work makes it clear that Mary could be claimed for apostolic leadership, without any implication that that position needed to be defended.[75] The clique of the Twelve is not yet fixed in tradition as the sole source of apostolic authority. Paul and Mary Magdalene in particular are also widely appealed to as sources of authoritative tradition in the early period.

The work of Ann Brock on the figures of Peter and Mary in early Christian tradition further supports this view.[76] She argues that the tradition of the Twelve and its connection with Peter is first forged in the Gospel of Luke but only slowly becomes widespread. The competition between Peter and Mary, on the other hand, had its roots in the pre-Pauline and pre-Gospel tradition. Moreover, the chronological and geographical spread of the tradition did not follow a single trajectory but can be found in widely dispersed and literarily unrelated literature. She did observe a tendency to reduce Mary Magalene's role when Peter's status was magnified (e.g., in the Gospel of Luke), while in texts where Mary Magdalene plays an important role, especially as witness to the resurrection, Peter is less prominent (e.g., in the Gospel of John). Explicit competition appears between them in later texts where the status of Mary Magdalene plays a prominent role. Texts where Peter is figured as the apostolic authority, on the other hand, "consistently do not present arguments supporting the role of female leaders; rather the role of women is effectively modeled in women's absences, silence or submission."[77] The notion of the Twelve is not a motif present in other literary conflicts between Peter and Mary. So it would seem to be the case in the *Gospel of Mary* as well. What we do find is that "Peter appears to be a pivotal figure in the polemic against women's leadership."[78]

---

[74] Hartenstein, *Die zweite Lehre,* 130–32.

[75] See ibid., 150. She argues that Mary's response to Peter and Andrew indicates that neither of them is willing to go so far as to suggest that she is lying. The effect of Mary's reply is rather to sharpen the point that Peter (and the other disciples—and readers) must either accept everything Mary has said or fundamentally deny that she is a disciple. Already by causing a rift among the disciples, Peter shows himself to be the guilty one.

[76] See Brock, "Authority, Politics, and Gender," esp. 143–48.

[77] See ibid., 16.

[78] Ibid., 210.

6. Who Can Be Relied upon to Preach the Gospel?

I would argue that the contrasting portrayal of the disciples in the *Gospel of Mary* is not aimed against the Twelve, nor to support gnostics against orthodox, nor visionaries against apostolic witnesses. The problem being addressed is rather that the *Gospel of Mary* was written at a time when the truth of Christian teaching could not be settled by appeal to a commonly accepted rule of faith or canon of authoritative Gospel literature, let alone an established leadership. So instead, the *Gospel of Mary* has to frame the issue as a matter of character: Who can be relied upon to preach the gospel? The standard method to distinguish a true prophet or teacher from a false one was by examining their character and behavior.[79] The *Gospel of Mary* argues for the truth of its teaching based on a contrast between Mary's character and Peter's.

The choice of these two characters was no accident. Early traditions that Mary saw the risen Lord and was an important follower of Jesus and witness to the resurrection no doubt played a role in choosing her to play a similar role in the *Gospel of Mary*. Peter, too, was a good candidate for his role because of his reputation for being impulsive, uncomprehending, and weak. For example, the Gospel of Mark records a scene where Jesus himself calls Peter "Satan" (Mark 8:31–33). Jesus had just predicted his death and suffering, and Peter had the temerity to tell Jesus he was wrong! Or again, Peter insists that even if everyone else abandons Jesus, he never will (Mark 14:29–31 and parallels)—just before he denies him not once, but three times (Mark 14:66–72 and parallels in Matthew). Jesus has to save Peter from drowning because Peter's faith is too weak (Matt 14:28–31). Even Paul had troubles with Peter, and accused him of acting like a hypocrite because he would change his behavior to suit his audience.[80] There are repeated examples in the early Gospel literature where Peter has just not quite understood what is going on (e.g., Mark 9:5–6; John 13:6–11; 18:10–11). The *Gospel of the Nazarenes* took a very harsh position and pronounced the final judgment that Peter "denied and swore and damned himself" (*Gos. Naz.* 19).

While widespread, this portrait of Peter is not the only one, of course. He is also the first to confess that Jesus is the Christ. Jesus calls him the "rock" upon which he will build his church and hands him the keys to God's realm (Matt 16:16–19). In the Gospel of John, Jesus says that Peter loves him more than the other, and he commissions him to "feed his sheep" (John 21:15–19).

---

[79] E.g., the *Didache*.

[80] See Gal 2:13. The Revised Standard Version diplomatically translates the Greek ὑποκρίσει as "insincerity" instead of "hypocrisy."

In later tradition, Peter is often used to authorize particular theological positions. Second Peter, for example, is an early second-century letter that was written in his name in order to claim Peter's authority to support the author's positions. The author of 2 Peter explicitly supports the idea of apostolic authority by calling upon the readers to remember "the commandment of the Lord and Savior through your apostles."[81] Peter was not always linked with the same position, however, and was in fact sometimes even used to authorize opposite sides of an issue. For example, Irenaeus uses him as a witness to the physical reality of Jesus' incarnation,[82] while in the *Apocalypse of Peter,* Peter receives special revelation from the Savior rejecting the incarnation and affirming that Jesus only seemed to have a body. Both Irenaeus and the *Apocalypse of Peter* appeal to Peter's witness to support their own (opposing) theological traditions.

My point here is that, while Peter will eventually become attached to the position supporting apostolic tradition as the basis for the patriarchal hierarchy of the church, in the early period he was more fluid as a character.[83] The *Gospel of Mary* did not choose him because he was already associated with a developed position on apostolic authority (or because he was portrayed as a leading representative of the Twelve) but because he was known to be full of bluster and misunderstanding. In the *Gospel of Mary* he is portrayed as a jealous and contentious character who cannot see beyond his own male pride and who clearly has not achieved inner stability and peace. Peter represents the folly of trusting that simply having heard the teaching of Jesus is enough to ensure that one has actually understood it. Andrew, as Peter's brother, seems to be guilty by association. To read more into the controversy would anachronistically assume a fixity of theological positions and hierarchical practices not yet in place.

Mary, on the other hand, was consistently represented as the faithful disciple. In the Gospels of Mark and Matthew, when the male disciples fled at the arrest of Jesus (Mark 14:50; Matt 26:56) and abandoned him at his crucifixion, women were present (Mark 15:40–41; Matt 27:55–56). It

---

[81] The letter also goes on to invoke Peter's authority against certain interpretations of Paul that the unknown author of the letter opposed (see 2 Pet 3:14–17).

[82] See *Haer.* 3.13.2: "How could Peter, to whom the Lord gave the testimony that flesh and blood had not revealed this to him but heaven, have been in ignorance?" referring to Matt 16:17.

[83] For excellent and more extensive discussion of Peter, see Raymond E. Brown et al., eds., *Peter in the New Testament: A Collaborative Assessment by Protestant and Roman Catholic Scholars* (Minneapolis: Augsburg; New York: Paulist, 1973); Terence V. Smith, *Petrine Controversies in Early Christianity: Attitudes towards Peter in Christian Writings of the First Two Centuries* (WUNT 2/15; Tübingen: Mohr Siebeck, 1985); and Brock, "Authority, Politics, and Gender."

was women who watched to see where the body was buried and who first went to the tomb and learned the message of the resurrection (Mark 15:47; 16:1–8; Matt 27:61; 28:1–10). They were commissioned by angels or by the Lord himself to bring the news to the male disciples.[84] Mary Magdalene is consistently represented as preeminent among these women in the canonical narratives and often is listed first. She accompanied Jesus throughout his ministry (Mark 15:40–41; Matt 27:55–56; Luke 8:1–3; John 19:25; *Gos. Phil.* 59.6–9), was present at his crucifixion (Mark 15:40–41; John 19:25),[85] and was a witness to the resurrection (Mark 16:1–8; Matt 28:1–7; Luke 24:1–10; John 20:1, 11–18). Indeed, she is portrayed as the first or among the first privileged to see and speak with the risen Lord (Matt 28:9–10; John 20:14–18; Mark 16:9). Among the earliest Christian art that survives is a portrait of Mary Magdalene with other women bringing spices to the tomb to anoint Jesus.[86] In the Gospel of John, the risen Jesus gives her special teaching and commissions her as an apostle to the apostles to bring them the good news (John 20:17).[87] It is therefore no surprise that Mary continues to figure as "the faithful woman disciple" in later literature.

The portrait of Mary Magdalene in the *Gospel of Mary* offers an alternative to sole reliance on apostolic witness as the source of authority. Although she, too, knew the historical Jesus, was a witness to the resurrection, and received instruction from the Savior, these experiences are not what set her apart from the others. Mary is clearly portrayed throughout the *Gospel* as an exemplary disciple. She does not falter when the Savior departs. She steps into his place after his departure, comforting, strengthening, and instructing the others. Her spiritual comprehension and spiritual maturity are demonstrated in her calm behavior and especially in her visionary experience. These at once provide evidence of her spiritual maturity

---

[84] It is interesting that Luke gives no account of the disciples fleeing, and he expands the group at the cross to include "acquaintances" as well as the women (Luke 23:49). Neither are the women commissioned by the angel at the tomb to tell the other disciples, and when they do report it, they are not believed (Luke 24:1–12). In John, again there is no account of the disciples fleeing, and "the beloved disciple" is placed at the cross, as well as women (John 19:25–26). But John is clear in making Mary Magdalene the first to discover the empty tomb, and the first to receive an appearance and commissioning from the risen Lord (John 20:1–2, 11–18).

[85] She was also said to be present at the entombment in Mark 15:47 and Matt 27:61.

[86] See Robert Milburn, *Early Christian Art and Architecture* (Berkeley and Los Angeles: University of California Press, 1988), 12; Haskins, *Mary Magdalene,* 58–63.

[87] In Mark 16:7 and Matt 28:7, angels commission Mary and the other women to carry the news of the resurrection.

and form the basis for her legitimate exercise of authority in instructing the other disciples. She does not teach in her own name but passes on the words of the Savior, calming the disciples, and turning their hearts toward the Good. Her character proves the truth of her teaching, and by extension authorizes the teaching of the *Gospel of Mary*—and it does so opposing her to those apostles who reject women's authority and preach another gospel, laying down laws beyond that which the Savior taught.

7. Conclusion

What effect does all this have on our understanding of the figuration of Mary Magdalene in the second century? First of all, like the figuration of other disciples, she is as much a type as an individual. That is, just as Peter is the "hothead" or Thomas the "doubter," Mary is the "faithful woman." The *Gospel of Mary* develops her role as a visionary and leading female disciple for its own ends: to legitimize its interpretation of Jesus' teaching, to support its theology more generally, and to argue for leadership based on spiritual maturity, not solely on apostolic transmission and never on sex-gender distinctions, rooted as they are in the perishable world. According to the *Gospel of Mary*, merely hearing or seeing Jesus, before or after the resurrection, was not enough to ensure that the gospel was preached in truth. It was precisely the traditions of Mary as a woman, as an exemplary disciple, a witness to the ministry of Jesus, a visionary of the glorified Jesus, and someone traditionally in contest with Peter, that made her the only figure who could play all the roles required to convey the messages and meaning of the *Gospel of Mary*. It was these characteristics that made her a figure around which controversy was sure to swirl.

Mary Magdalene in the *Acts of Philip*

François Bovon

Harvard University

1. The Name Mary

Sura 19 of the Qur'an gives Mary, Jesus' mother, the honorary epithet "sister of Aaron."[1] A few Jewish texts of late antiquity and the Middle Ages merge the Virgin Mary with Mary Magdalene.[2] Such connections were made possible and even attractive because of the similarity in names. First I would like to reflect on the several forms of the name Mary and then examine the persons of that same name.

Miriam is the Hebrew name.[3] It is applied to the sister of Aaron and Moses. The Septuagint regularly translates this name with Μαριάμ. Philo follows this usage,[4] while Josephus never uses this term and instead calls the sister of Aaron and Moses Μαριάμμη.[5] The New Testament manuscripts do not witness the name Μαριάμμη, preferring Μαριάμ or Μαρία for Jesus' mother, the woman from Magdala, and the several other Marys.[6] We have,

---

[1] See Jaroslav Pelikan, *Mary through the Centuries* (New Haven: Yale University Press, 1996), 72–73.

[2] See R. Travers Herford, *Christianity in Talmud and Midrash* (London: Williams & Norgate, 1903), 355, 358. I thank my colleague Jon Levenson, who helped me in this matter. One finds the same assimilation in a Coptic homily probably from the sixth century C.E.; see Pseudo-Cyril of Jerusalem, *Homily on the Dormition* (E. A. Wallis Budge, *Miscellaneous Coptic Texts in the Dialect of Upper Egypt* [London: British Museum, 1915], 630). I thank Dr. Ann Graham Brock for this information.

[3] On the Hebrew name, its origin, structure, and meaning, see Scott C. Layton, *Archaic Features of Canaanite Personal Names in the Hebrew Bible* (HSM 47; Atlanta: Scholars Press,1990), 183–86. I thank Professor Jo Ann Hackett for this reference.

[4] See Philo of Alexandria, *Leg.* 1.76; 2.66; 2.103; *Agr.* 80–81; *Contempl.* 87.

[5] Or Μαριάμη according to manuscript evidence; see Abraham Schalit, *Namenwörterbuch zu Flavius Josephus* (suppl. 1 of *A Complete Concordance to Flavius Josephus;* Leiden: Brill, 1968), s.v. Besides the sister of Moses and Aaron, Josephus knows six different Μαριάμ(μ)η. He mentions also once a Μαρία (*War* 6.201).

[6] The author of Luke-Acts uses Μαριάμ for Jesus' mother. In the only genitive use of this name he prefers Μαριᾶς; he calls Mary Magdalene Μαρία, and the sister of

therefore, three different spellings in Greek. The Coptic authors, translators, and scribes use the same three forms of the name known from the Greek. The Latin translators of the Bible used only the name Maria when they refer to the sister of Aaron and Moses, Jesus' mother, or Jesus' friend.

I spent an afternoon in the Widener Library poring over the venerable Pape, *Wörterbuch der griechischen Eigennamen,* Bechtel, *Personennamen,* and Preisigke, *Namenbuch* (with its supplement *Onomasticon alterum papyrologicum*), the more recent *Lexicon of Greek Personal Names* according to regions (two volumes so far), Kajava's *Roman Female Praenomina* as well as Kajanto's *Onomastic in the Early Christian Inscriptions of Rome and Carthage,* Jones and Whitehorne's *Register of Oxyrhynchites,* and Tcherikover and Fuks's *Corpus papyrorum judaicarum.*[7]

What I found was an intriguing thread. In Jewish inscriptions and papyri the names Μαρία and Μαριάμ are attested in the time of the Roman Empire.[8] With variations in Greek spelling, the name Μάρεια can be applied

---

Martha Μαριάμ. But we must be careful: the textual evidence can vary from one manuscript to the other. Matthew can use Μαριάμ or Μαρία for the same person. The same is true of John.

[7] Wilhelm Pape and Gustav Benseler, eds., *Wörterbuch der griechischen Eigennamen* (2 vols.; repr. of 3d ed.; Orbis litterarum; Graz: Akademische Druck- und Verlagsanstalt, 1959); Friedrich Bechtel, *Die historischen Personennamen des Griechischen bis zur Kaiserzeit* (Halle: Niemeyer, 1917); Friedrich Preisigke and Enno Littmann, *Namenbuch* (Heidelberg: Selbstverlag des Herausgebers, 1922); Daniele Foraboschi, *Onomasticon alterum papyrologicum: Supplemento al Namenbuch di F. Preisigke* (TDSA 16, Serie papirologica 2; Milan-Varese: Istituto editoriale cisalpino, 1971); Peter Marshall Fraser and Elaine Matthews, eds., *A Lexicon of Greek Personal Names* (Oxford: Clarendon, 1987–); Mika Kajava, *Roman Female Praenomina: Studies in the Nomenclature of Roman Women* (AIRF 14; Rome: Institutum romanum Finlandiae, 1995); Iiro Kajanto, *Onomastic in the Early Christian Inscriptions of Rome and Carthage* (AIRF 2/1; Helsinki: Helsinki University Press, 1963); Brian W. Jones and J. E. G. Whitehorne, *Register of Oxyrhynchites 30 B.C.—A.D. 96* (ASP 25; Chico, Calif.: Scholars Press, 1983); Victor A. Tcherikover and Alexander Fuks, eds., *Corpus papyrorum judaicarum* (3 vols.; Cambridge: Harvard University Press, 1957–64); see also August Fick, *Die griechischen Personennamen nach ihrer Bildung erklärt mit den Namensystemen verwandter Sprachen verglichen und systematisch geordnet* (Göttingen: Vandenhoeck & Ruprecht, 1874); Olli Salomies, *Die römischen Vornamen: Studien zur römischen Namengebung* (Commentationes humanarum litterarum 82; Helsinki: Societas scientiarum fennica, 1987). I would like to thank Eldon J. Epp, who gave me the titles of some of these works.

[8] The name Μαρία is present in two Jewish papyri of the beginning of the second century C.E. and one Egyptian grave inscription; see Tcherikover and Fuks, *Corpus papyrorum judaicarum,* vol. 2, nos. 223 and 227, vol. 3, no. 1535: Μαρία

to the Lake close to Alexandria (Lake Mareotis) and to the city on its shore. Μαρία appears also as the name of an island along the African coast of the Red Sea. Μαριαμμία (sometimes written Μαριάμμη) exists in Syria as a city known later as the metropolis of a bishop.[9] But as a name for a woman neither Μαρία nor Μαριάμ are Greek. If they are attested as such, it is in later records and under Jewish, Christian, or perhaps Latin influence. Of course Μαρία has been very popular in Greece through the present, but under Christian influence.

One must recall that the Greeks and the Jews had a simpler onomastic system than the Romans, in having no *praenomina* nor *cognomina*. To distinguish between two women with the same name they indicated—as you know—the name of the father or the husband.

Let's turn now to the Latin onomastic. Normally in Rome a woman was named according to her *nomen gentilicium* (name of her *gens, grosso modo* our last name): Cornelia for a woman from the *gens* of the Cornelii.[10] If she was of a noble family she could keep the name of her family instead of taking the one of her husband. There was an evolution in the Latin onomastic system. While the *nomen* had been for a long time the only name for a woman, a *praenomen* and even a *cognomen* developed thereafter. The Latin Maria represents the feminine form of the *nomen gentilicium* Marius.[11] Incidentally—to complicate the matter—the name Marius existed among the Oscs, a people of South Italy (Campania),[12] conquered early by the Romans.[13] I cannot discern if the Oscs used *praenomina* and if the feminine Maria as a *praenomen* is attested among the Oscs. The Latin Maria was probably pronounced Mária because Latin cannot accept an accent on the

---

Ἀβιήτου, who died March 31, 116 C.E. (no. 227); Μαρία Δημᾶτος, who died February 28, 116 C.E. (no. 223); a Maria from Antinoopolis daughter of Phamsothis (inscr. 1535).

[9] See Wilhelm Enßlin, "Maria," PW 14:1712–13.

[10] More precision would follow with the name of her father or of her husband or both.

[11] In the second century B.C.E. two sisters of C. Marius bore the name Maria; one became the wife of M. Gratidius, the other the mother of C. Lucius; in the fourth century C.E. a Maria is known as the wife of the emperor Honorius; see Ruth Albrecht, "Maria," *DNP* 7:887–90.

[12] "Peuple de langue sabellique de l'Italie ancienne, établi en Campanie, influencé par les Grecs et soumis par les Samnites, mais qui conserva sa langue jusqu'au ~ 1ᵉʳ siècle" (Paul Robert and Alain Rey, eds., *Le Petit Robert 2: Dictionnaire universel des noms propres, alphabétique et analogique, illustré en couleurs* [Paris: Le Robert, 1991], s.v.).

[13] See Salomies, *Die römischen Vornamen*, 77–78.

penultimate if this syllable is short.[14] In such cases the accent goes back to the previous syllable. But in the early Roman empire Maria was introduced as *praenomen* under Jewish influence.

Bertrand Bouvier, my co-editor of the *Acts of Philip,* reminded me of a particular piece of philological evidence. When a Greek word ends with a consonant, the consonant can only be ν, ρ, or ς. Any name ending with another consonant therefore sounds foreign or barbaric. And that would be the case of Μαριάμ. This very fact may explain the two other forms of Mary, namely, Μαρία and Μαριάμμη, chosen perhaps to erase the impression of strangeness, the foreign character of the name.[15]

In my view, to disentangle the changing usage of the name, more work must be done, and I would suggest that the following criteria be applied. First, scholars should consider the language in which the name occurs; second, they should respect the period in which the text being considered was composed; third, they should establish the geographic location of the document; fourth, researchers should examine the class or social milieu of the author; and fifth, they should understand the prevalent intellectual or religious traditions.[16]

Why, for example, does Josephus choose the name Μαριάμμη for the sister of Moses and Aaron, and why does he *not* follow the translation chosen by the Septuagint? Is it because he desires to avoid the barbaric character of that name and perhaps follows a hellenizing Jewish tradition? Or as all the other Μαριάμμη he mentions are Jewish princesses, does he wish to underline the aristocratic character of the sister of Aaron and Moses? The deliberate choice of Μαρία or Μαριάμμη expresses in my view an assimilation into Greek language and culture.

2. The Two Marys

If we turn now from the names to the person,[17] there is evidence that the same person may have received each of the three forms of the name. The mother of Jesus is called Μαριάμ or Μαρία in the New Testament,

[14] If today we say María (accent on the *i*) in Italian, it is an exception under Greek influence of the Byzantine period. The same is true for Lucia, pronounced today Lucía.

[15] It must be added finally that Μαριάμμη was spelled sometimes Μαριάμη or Μαριάμνη, as one can see from the manuscript traditions.

[16] See N. C. Cohen, "The Proper Name 'Miriam' in Greek and Latin Transliteration" [Hebrew with English summary], *Leš* 38 (1974): 170–80; Stephen J. Shoemaker, "Mary and the Discourse of Orthodoxy: Early Christian Identity and the Ancient Dormition Legends" (Ph.D. diss., Duke University, 1997), 170–97.

[17] As it is known from Josephus, *War* 2.439; 5.170; and 7.1, Μαριάμμη was also the name of a tower in Jerusalem.

Μαριάμμη in three passages of the *Protevangelium of James* (according to the most ancient manuscript, P.Bod. V).[18] The assignment of names to Mary Magdalene is identical.[19] She is called Μαρία ἡ Μαγδαληνή in Matt 27:56; Μαριὰμ ἡ Μαγδαληνή a few verses later in Matt 27:61; and Μαριάμμη in the *Gospel of Mary,* Hippolytus *Haer.* 5.1.7, Origen *Cels.* 5.62, and, in a Latin form, Priscillian's *Apologeticum* 1.[20]

Is there a tendency in the *catholica* to call Jesus' mother Μαρία and a pattern in nonorthodox communities for referring to Jesus' friend as Μαριάμμη? Probably not. When Mary Magdalene is designated Μαρία, a reference to her hometown Magdala often clearly identifies who she is.

---

[18] See Émile de Strycker, *La forme la plus ancienne du Protévangile de Jacques* (SHG 33; Brussels: Société des Bollandistes, 1961), 315–16.

[19] In recent years the secondary literature on Mary Magdalene has grown enormously; for ancient bibliography, see François Bovon, "Le privilège pascal de Marie-Madeleine," *NTS* 30 (1984): 50–62; in English in idem, *New Testament Traditions and Apocryphal Narratives* (trans. J. Haapiseva-Hunter; PTMS 36; Allison Park, Pa.: Pickwick, 1994), 147–57, 228–35; for more recent works, see Renate Schmid, *Maria Magdalena in gnostischen Schriften* (Material-Edition 29; Munich: Arbeitsgemeinschaft für Religions- und Weltanschauungsfragen, 1990); J. Kevin Coyle, "Mary Magdalene in Manichaeism?" *Mus* 104 (1991): 39–55; Maddalena Scopello, "Marie-Madeleine et la tour: *Pistis et sophia,*" in *Figures du Nouveau Testament chez les Pères* (CBiPa 3; Strasbourg: Centre d'analyse et de documentation patristiques, 1991), 179–96; Carla Ricci, *Maria di Magdal e le molte alter: Donne sul cammino di Gesù* (Naples: D'Auria, 1991); Susan Haskins, *Mary Magdalene: Myth and Metaphor* (New York: Harcourt Brace, 1993); Hannele Koivunen, *Madonna ja huora* [in Finnish; based on the author's dissertation "The Woman Who Understood Completely: A Semiotic Analysis of the Mary Magdalene Myth in the Gnostic Gospel of Mary," University of Helsinki, 1994] (Helsinki: Otava, 1995); Antti Marjanen, *The Woman Jesus Loved: Mary Magdalene in the Nag Hammadi Library and Related Documents* (Nag Hammadi and Manichaean Studies 40; Leiden: Brill, 1996); Ingrid Maisch, *Maria Magdalena zwischen Verachtung und Verehrung: Das Bild einer Frau im Spiegel der Jahrhunderte* (Freiburg im Breisgau: Herder, 1996); Shoemaker, "Mary and the Discourse of Orthodoxy"; Frédéric Amsler, *Acta Philippi: Commentarius* (CCSA 12; Turnhout: Brepols, 1999), 312–17; Silke Petersen, *"Zerstört die Werke der Weiblichkeit!" Maria Magdalena, Salome und andere Jüngerinnnen Jesu in christlich-gnostischen Schriften* (Nag Hammadi and Manichaean Studies 48; Leiden: Brill, 1999). More bibliography in Petersen, *"Zerstört die Werke der Weiblichkeit!"* 351–71.

[20] There are of course other Marys in the New Testament: Mary, Martha's sister (Luke 10:38–42; John 11:1–12:8), merged in the *Acts of Philip* with Mary Magdalene; Mary of James (Matt 27:56; Mark 15:40; 16:1; Luke 24:10; see Matt 28:1); Mary of Joses (Mark 15:40, 47); Mary of Clopas (John 19:25); Mary, mother of John Mark (Acts 12:12); Mary who worked hard (Rom 16:6).

The figure of Μαριάμνη (spelled sometimes Μαριάμμη in one or two manuscripts,[21] particularly the oldest one, P) present in the *Acts of Philip* cannot be Jesus' mother (mentioned once or twice as Μαρία in the text, *Acts Phil.* 6.13 [V and A], *Acts Phil. Mart.* 35.6 [Γ, absent from Θ and Δ]), because if so, Philip would be Jesus' uncle! This figure is not connected with Jesus' birth but with his ministry and resurrection. The woman, it is my contention, is Mary Magdalene. I will insist on such a presence of Mary Magdalene in the *Acts of Philip* because this evidence has been neglected and because of the new manuscripts recently discovered and edited.[22]

3. Mariamne in the Acts of Philip

To be clear, I am not interested here in the reconstruction of the historical figure of Mary Magdalene, but in her portrayal in literary texts, particularly in the *Acts of Philip*.[23]

3.1. The Presence of Mariamne

Mariamne is quite present in the second half of the *Acts of Philip*.[24] Philip the apostle is the leader of the small group of missionaries sent by the resurrected Savior. Twice when the trio, Bartholomew, Mariamne, and himself, meets a formidable dragon, Philip remains calm while Mariamne is frightened (*Acts Phil.* 11.5), and he performs the victorious exorcism (*Acts Phil.* 9.1–5 and 11.6–7). After the governor's wife, Nicanora, has made the acquaintance of Mariamne, it is Philip who takes the leading position (*Acts Phil. Mart.* 11 [V]). On another occasion he celebrates the Eucharist and gives her communion, not the other way around (*Acts Phil.* 11.1 and 10). Nevertheless, as Ann Graham Brock pointed out in her dissertation,[25]

---

[21] I am referring to the sigla used in the edition of François Bovon, Bertrand Bouvier, and Frédéric Amsler, *Acta Philippi: Textus* (CCSA 11; Turnhout: Brepols, 1999). P is the *Parisinus gr. 881;* A is Athos, *Xenophontos 32;* V is the *Vaticanus gr. 824;* G is *Atheniensis 346;* Γ, Δ, and Θ represent the three different Greek recensions of the *Martyrdom of Philip,* the last part of the *Acts of Philip.*

[22] See n. 21 above for the reference to the edition.

[23] See Bovon, "Le privilège pascal," 50–62 (in English, Bovon, *New Testament Traditions,* 147–57, 228–35).

[24] Mariamne is absent from the first half of the *Acts of Philip* (*Acts Phil.* 1–7), which leads scholars to believe that this work is a composite one and that *Acts Phil.* 1–7 are of another origin, probably related to Philip the evangelist (see Acts 6–8).

[25] Ann Graham Brock, "Authority, Politics, and Gender in Early Christianity: Mary, Peter, and the Portrayal of Leadership" (Ph.D. diss., Harvard University, 2000), 176 n. 1.

Mariamne is part of the group (see *Acts Phil. Mart.* 7 [V] and 26 [V]) and carries with Philip and Bartholomew the prestigious title οἱ ἀπόστολοι (see *Acts Phil.* 8.16 and 21; 13.1–2.4).

3.2. Mariamne's Healing Activity

At two occasions in this text Mariamne is connected with a healing activity. First, while the apostolic group arrives in the city of Ophiorumos, Philip, like an itinerant physician, looks for a place to exercise his art. He shares with Mariamne the satisfaction of finding an abandoned clinic or dispensary (ἰατρεῖον) and invites her discreetly to install the group in that place that will become, he says, a "spiritual dispensary" (τὸ πνευματικὸν τοῦτο ἰατρεῖον, *Acts Phil.* 13.4).

Second, in the following act, *Acts Phil.* 14, the reader meets an aged man Stachys,[26] who has suffered blindness for forty years, but a dream has brought him to the apostles. Imitating Jesus' enigmatic gesture, Philip will use saliva to cure this blindness. But different from the Markan Jesus (Mark 8:22–26), Philip does not use his own saliva but dips his finger into Mariamne's mouth and extracts *her* saliva as a curative unguent. Alas, the first readers of the *Acts of Philip* could not bear that narrative, and the end of the episode has been expurgated in the only manuscript that has preserved this story (A). Like the evangelists Matthew and Luke, who considered Mark's episode too shocking to accept, a reader has torn away the folio between folios 87 and 88.

3.3. Mariamne's Teaching Activity

Philip is the apostle entrusted with preaching the good news, but the reader encounters several episodes in which Mariamne is a powerful, charismatic speaker and not simply an audience. In the martyrdom story, the apostolic group is active in Ophiorumos. The apostles have expanded their mission: they now use the house of Stachys as a gathering place where the guests can hear the Christian message, and Mariamne is represented as being posted at the entrance of the house as a sort of hostess, inviting the public in to hear the good news.

The martyrdom story of the *Acts of Philip* is preserved in three recensions. One recension (Θ) has, in an orthodox way,[27] eradicated Mariamne's

---

[26] Stachys's name and story have been preserved till today in the *Synaxarion* of the Orthodox Church for the Feast of Saint Philip celebrated November 14; see Hippolyte Delehaye, *Synaxarium ecclesiae constantinopolitanae,* 117 and 1165 (index).

[27] As historians we can use these categories for the time of the Byzantine compilers and scribes.

teaching role, while another (Γ),[28] more open here to another orientation, recognizes her teaching activity (*Acts Phil. Mart.* 3).[29] But even this approbation is not without limitation: the recension Γ restricts Mariamne's role to calling the visitors to enter and to listen to Philip. It is probable that in the original form of the story, Mariamne was the legitimate missionary to women while Philip was the evangelist for men. An invective formulated by future pagan opponents accuses Mariamne of following men and of deceiving women (*Acts Phil. Mart.* 19 [Γ and Δ]), which I understand to mean that Mariamne is guilty both of fraternizing with Philip and Bartholomew and of preaching the encratite private life to women.

There is a confirmation of Mariamne's preaching activity in her encounter with Nicanora, the governor's wife (*Acts Phil. Mart.* 9). Mariamne is not content to relate to Nicanora via Philip's proselytizing, but she herself begins to profess to her listener a serious doctrinal teaching. She communicates the following message to Nicanora: You have fallen away from the divine family house and succumbed to the demonic power of the snake. You are guilty of having forgotten your origins, your Father in heaven, and your spiritual Mother. If you wake up, however, you will receive illumination. Nicanora has two reasons to exult: by Mariamne's κήρυγμα she has been spiritually saved and physically cured (*Acts Phil. Mart.* 10).[30]

3.4. Mariamne's Liturgical Activity

At several occasions the *Acts of Philip* presents Mariamne sharing ministerial responsibilities in the community. She is said to have prepared the bread and the salt for the communion[31] while Martha was serving the crowds[32] (*Acts Phil.* 8.2; in this ascetic text the wine of the communion is not mentioned).[33] At the very beginning of the Christian movement, at

---

[28] Manuscript V presents the text of recension Γ, manuscript A the text of recension Θ.

[29] The third recension Δ starts later in *Acts Phil. Mart.* 17.

[30] Manuscript V reads "the preaching of my fathers" and A "your [pl.] preaching." I suggest that the original meaning was the apostolic teaching, delivered here by Mariamne, which coincides with the faith of Nicanora's ancestors, the Jewish patriarchs.

[31] Women were present and active in the community of the Therapeutae; bread and salt were also the food of the Therapeutae described by Philo of Alexandria, *Contempl.* 37 and 73; see the quotations and summary of Philo's works in Eusebius of Caesarea, *Hist. eccl.* 2.17.

[32] Is the word "crowds" an ecclesiological expression, like the "many" in the Dead Sea Scrolls (see for example 1QS 6.1–7.27) and in Mark 10:45?

[33] The text presupposes that Mary Magdalene and Mary of Bethany are the same person.

the time of the sending of the apostles, her actions evoke the Last Supper, and to have participated in the preparation of the Last Supper confers authority and prestige to Mariamne, of course. There is an echo of this claim and at the same time a criticism of it in one of the ancient church orders, the so-called *Ecclesiastical Constitution of the Apostles*.[34] In a short narrative the "orthodox" Jesus of the *Constitution* forbids both Mary and Martha to conduct the celebration of the Eucharist.

Similar in importance is Mariamne's baptismal activity. Twice the text affirms that Mariamne was responsible for the baptism of women, and this does not represent an exception but the rule, as the imperfect tense indicates: "Philip baptized the men and Mariamne the women" (*Acts Phil.* 14.9; see also *Acts Phil. Mart.* 2 [Θ]).[35] We know that women were active in the celebration of baptism in the orthodox communities: in some regions of the East deaconesses had the responsibility to perform an unction with oil[36] and to hold out the requisite white garments to the newly baptized women at the moment of their ascent from the water.[37] But these responsibilities were limited. The baptism itself was performed by a man, the bishop or later the priest. Such is not the case here: Mariamne carries the whole responsibility of the baptism of women.

3.5. Mariamne's Suffering

Mariamne does not escape the persecution that reaches Philip. Nicanora's husband, the governor with the terrible name of Tyranno-gnophos, is furious at the new ascetical, encratite lifestyle of his wife. Not without reason he accuses the Christian apostles for the changes that his wife embraces, and he imagines some magical tricks. The apostolic trio is arrested, taken under custody in a pagan temple, and then subjected to a bodily search (*Acts Phil. Mart.* 14–20). A miracle protects Mariamne from eventual shame during her humiliation: the moment the soldiers try to strip away her clothing, the form of her body is transformed. One recension reads that a discreet cloud took her away from the indiscreet eyes of her enemies [Γ]. The two other forms of the text [Θ and Δ], probably closer to the original, say that her body was transformed to a κιβωτὸς ὑελίνη, a "shrine of glass." This term κιβωτός is extremely interesting because it is the same term that the Septuagint

---

34 See *Ecclesiastical Constitution of the Apostles* 26; and Bovon, Bouvier, and Amsler, *Acta Philippi: Textus,* 240 n. 5.

35 Compare Firmilian's letter to Cyprian in Cyprian, *Epistle* 75.10.

36 See *Const. ap.* 3.16; *Didascalia apostolorum* 16.

37 Aimé Georges Martimort, *Deaconesses: An Historical Study* (trans. K. D. Whitehead; San Francisco: Ignatius, 1986), 43–44, 52–57.

uses for the ark of Noah (Gen 6:14–9:18) and the ark of the covenant (Exod 25:9–21 et passim). It is also the term that the Christian liturgy applies in a typological way to the Virgin Mary, referring to her as the receptacle of God's presence.

For the author of this segment of the *Acts of Philip,* as for many Christians of late antiquity, men and women can appear in three different forms: in the dress of sinful luxury, in the modest clothing of faith, and in the glorious body of the resurrection. What happens for Mariamne is a temporary manifestation of her resurrectional status. Her suffering is therefore not an inexorable ending. During the violent aggression of the governor, she is allowed to put on her dress of light, although for just a short time, but it is time enough to realize the power and the presence of the divine glory. After this transformation from humility to glory there is a return to her human condition; as the Jesus of the canonical gospels is finally back on earth "alone" (Mark 9:8 par.), so too Mariamne recuperates her "first type" (*Acts Phil. Mart.* 25 [Θ] and 32).

Human existence is limited in time, and death remains inexorable. The *Acts of Philip* takes this reality seriously, and without mentioning martyrdom, twice the text announces Mariamne's death. Here the author is concerned with a special form of funeral for Mariamne. An order is given by the agonizing Philip to place her coffin in the River Jordan (*Acts Phil. Mart.* 31 [A] and 36), and this is a mysterious affirmation for two reasons. First, to my knowledge there is no other text locating Mariamne's death in Palestine. The Bible, however, mentions Miriam's burial at Kadesh (Num 20:1), a place that our author may have imagined not far from the River Jordan. Second, the location of her tomb in a river is also exceptional. I know only of one other case, Alaric I, king of the Visigoths, who died at Cosenza (Italy) in 410 C.E. and was buried by his soldiers in the River Busento.

3.6. Mariamne's Manly Faith and Male Clothing

Several ancient Christian texts describe the role of Mary Magdalene during the critical days of Jesus' death and resurrection. Preserved in a Coptic and an Ethiopic version, the *Epistula apostolorum,* for example, underlines the effort of three women to convince the disciples of the reality of their Lord's resurrection.[38] Both versions of this text explicitly name Mary in this context (the Ethiopic version underlines the priority of Mary Magdalene). Building on the same tradition, the *Manichaean Psalms* praise Mary, called Marihama (last letter not clear), for having brought together the fleeing disciples like a fisherman captures fish in his

---

[38] *Epistula apostolorum* 10–11.

net.[39] The *Acts of Philip* offers a full picture of this scene and confirms the vitality of this widespread tradition.

I first need to situate this passage of the *Acts of Philip* in the manuscript tradition. We cannot here rely on our major manuscript, the *Xenophontos 32,* because the gesture of a censor has violently extracted twenty-four folios. We possess the short version of the *Vaticanus 824,* but it is not so useful because its scribe also has applied a kind of censorship by avoiding much of the compromising material. The most valuable witness of a more complete version remains therefore the manuscript *Atheniensis 346* (G).

Acts Phil. 8, the beginning of the ancient Acts, depicts the comforting role of Mariamne among Jesus' disciples after the resurrection. The apostles are called together by the resurrected Savior, and Mariamne is among them (as Jesus' appearance to Mary Magdalene is part of the New Testament resurrection stories). She is said to have carried then the list of countries where the disciples will be sent, the ἀναγραφὴ τῶν χωρῶν (*Acts Phil.* 8.2 [G]), and in this way fills the function of special assistant to the Savior, a kind of chief of staff. Mariamne is also described as the sister of the apostle Philip. Because of this kinship she is asked by the Savior to take care of her brother, who is anxious at the prospect of his dangerous mission to the Greeks. She is even urged to travel with him and to defend virtue, and *Acts Phil.* 8 [G] represents Philip as weak and Mariamne as strong.

This is an ancient concept. One of the ancients, Plato, expressed his conviction that occasionally a man can be weak and a woman strong.[40] For this philosopher and many after him the categories of male and female were not neutral, the first connoted positively, the second negatively. According to *Acts Phil.* 8 [G] Philip as a man has a female faith and attitude, and spiritually, Mariamne expresses herself like a male facing the hostile world: "And the Savior told her: 'I know that you are good and brave in your soul and blessed among women. A feminine spirit has entered Philip while the male and courageous spirit is in you'" (*Acts Phil.* 8.3 [G]). Mariamne owes these qualities to the Savior's favor, being the object of a special calling (*Acts Phil.* 8.3–4 [G]). Her duty to her faith is also immense. *Acts Phil.* 8.3 affirms that the apostolic mission and her part in it involve nothing less than "the sufferings of martyrdom and the redemption of the whole world."

---

[39] Psalms of Heracleides, "There Were Ten Virgins," in C. R. C. Allberry, ed., *A Manichaean Psalm-Book: Part II* (Manichaean Manuscripts in the Chester Beatty Collection 2; Stuttgart: Kohlhammer, 1938), 192 lines 21–22.

[40] See Plato, *Resp.* 5.1 (453–456, part. 455d). I thank Stanley B. Marrow, who helped me locate this passage.

Few ancient Christian texts describe so vividly what this commission-ing implies. In *Acts Phil.* 8 [G] the Savior organizes Mariamne's enterprise and counts on its success. He gives her the following practical advice: "You, Mariamne, change your gown and your outward appearance. Put off all that in your form resembles a woman, in particular your summer dress [a rare word is used here: τὸ θέριστον]. Do not let your fringe be dragged on the ground, do not twist it, but cut it; then walk together with your brother Philip to the city called Ophiorumos, which is understood as the 'promenade of the snakes'" (*Acts Phil.* 8.4 [G]).

A theological explanation is given for the necessity of this change. From the beginning of the world there has been hostility—the text seems to defend an unusual position here—between Adam and Eve (and not between Eve and the Serpent). This hostility gave the Serpent the oppor-tunity to revolt against Adam and to befriend Eve. The result was Adam being deceived by his wife. For Mariamne to lose the feminine form is to abandon Eve's appearance. It can only be beneficial. When Mariamne enters into the city, the snakes will see her transformed (*Acts Phil.* 8.4). The author explains then in an obscure paragraph that the skin of the Serpent has to be identified with its venom—a reality that polluted Eve—and that this kind of original sin was then communicated from generation to gen-eration starting with Cain. The author concludes with a dogmatic sentence: "Therefore, Mariamne, flee away from Eve's poverty and be rich in your-self" (*Acts Phil.* 8.4 [G]).

3.7. Mariamne As Sister and Twin

The notion of sisterhood plays a double role in the plot, first as a phys-ical sister, second as a spiritual twin. Mariamne is introduced as Philip's sister. She is later presented as the twin sister of Nicanora. Behind Mariamne there is another sister, Miriam, the sister of Aaron and Moses, called Mari-amme by Josephus. Even if implicit, such a typology is present in the text. As Miriam, Philip's sister participates in the salvific exodus. As Miriam she has a ministerial responsibility. Just as Miriam leads the choir of the women while Moses sings with the men of Israel after the victorious crossing of the Red Sea,[41] so Mariamne in the *Acts of Philip* baptizes the women while her brother Philip baptizes the men. Interestingly Philo affirms that the com-munity of the Therapeutae has taken over this distribution in their liturgy.[42]

---

[41] See J. Doignon, "Miryam et son tambourin dans la prédication et l'archéolo-gie occidentale au IVe siècle," in *StPatr* 4 (ed. F. L. Cross; TU 79; Berlin: Akademie-Verlag, 1961), 71–77. I thank my colleague Nicholas Constas for this bib-liographic reference.

[42] See Philo of Alexandria, *Agr.* 80–81; *Contempl.* 87.

Sisterhood is the adequate relationship for ascetic Christians, because it is a feminine companionship without the risk of sexuality. A mother is *per definitionem* the opposite of virgin. A daughter implies the intimate intercourse of her parents.

It is possible that there were two diverging traditions in the first centuries of Christian thought regarding Philip and the women around him, one with his daughters (Clement of Alexandria, *Strom.* 3.52.5, is very pleased to infer from Acts 21:9 that Philip with his daughters was not opposed to marriage), and another with his sister (this ascetical tradition is present here in the *Acts of Philip*). As Christ of the Fourth Gospel entrusts his mother to the beloved disciple, so the Savior of the *Acts of Philip* entrusts the apostle Philip to his sister. It is not by chance that in the church the terms *sister* and *brother* became terms for several dimensions of a non-sexual relationship between male and female Christians. Spouses in late antiquity who decided to interrupt marital relationship and live ascetically choose the terms *brother* and *sister* to explain their new relationship.

The categories sister and brother did more than eliminate the suspicion of sexual attraction. They were also a convenient metaphor for a spiritual kinship. Beyond the relationship of brother and sister, the term "twin" suggested such a deeper kinship. As an example, Judas Thomas is considered as the twin of Jesus in the *Gospel of Thomas* and the *Acts of Thomas*.[43] This is the term used in the *Acts of Philip* to represent the spiritual bondage between the elect. Inside the true community, the believers are not only "so to speak" brothers and sisters, but "really" brothers and sisters,[44] not at the despicable level of the flesh but at the respectable level of the spirit.

Again this theory is not a Christian invention, but the appropriation of a Hellenic concept. The Greeks developed two opposite views on humanity. On one side they claim with Pindar, "different is the race of the humans, different is the race of the God"; on the other they affirm, with Plato, that the true human beings are related as members of the same spiritual family (συγγένεια).[45] Mariamne and Nicanora feel close to one another not only because they are both of Hebraic origin, speaking the same language, but because they share the same spiritual bondage, they are "twins" in the spirit of the Savior: σὺ ἀδελφή μου εἶ· μία μήτηρ ἠγέννησεν ἡμᾶς διδύμους (*Acts Phil. Mart.* 9 [Γ]).

Ann Graham Brock discusses in her dissertation the way in which certain traditions concerning Mary Magdalene have been appropriated by

---

[43] *Gospel of Thomas* Prologue; *Acts of Thomas* 31 and 39.

[44] On the *virgines subintroductae,* see Wolfgang Schrage, *Der erste Brief an die Korinther* (EKKNT 7; Zurich: Benziger, 1991–), 2:153, 208.

[45] Pindar, *Nem.* 6.1; Plato, *Prot.* 322a.

orthodox groups and applied to Mary the mother.[46] The portrayal of Mariamne in the *Acts of Philip* makes evident that a symmetrical appropriation
took place in the other direction. Titles, metaphors, and functions applied to
the mother in patristic texts appear here as characteristic of Mariamne. *Acts
Phil.* 8.3 applies the highest epithet εὐλογημένη ἐν γυναιξίν (see also Jdt
13:18) to Mariamne, while Luke applies it to Mary the mother (Luke 1:42).
At a critical moment, as we have seen, she is transformed into a κιβωτός, a
"chest," an "ark," the place of the divine presence, a category commonly
applied to the Virgin Mary.[47] She is finally the counterpart or the antitype
of Eve and through her faith and courage she undoes the sin that Eve has
introduced into the world (an argument that Justin Martyr and Irenaeus
apply to the Virgin Mary).[48]

4. Mariamne and the Feminine Ministry

What is new in the long text of the *Xenophontos 32,* compared with
the short text of the *Vaticanus graecus 824* [V], is a long tour of hell in
Acts Phil. 1. A young man resurrected by Philip tells the story of his trav-
els in the underworld. He has been guided to several places of
punishment where he can ask his *angelus interpres* questions. The punishments that are described are those inflicted on orthodox Christians,
mainly ecclesiastical leaders, who had criticized the encratite movement.
They receive their punishment because they have slandered the ministers
of the marginalized community. Lists of the different categories of ministry
are mentioned. They must reflect the ecclesiastical and sociological reality of the marginal community. Three categories, each of two pairs, are
prominent: the eunuchs and the virgins, the deacons and deaconesses, the
priests and the priestesses (*Acts Phil.* 1.12). From this list it is clear that
the encratite community that is behind *Acts Phil.* 1 vindicated women's

---

[46] See Brock, "Authority, Politics, and Gender," 183–99; Petersen, *"Zerstört die
Werke der Weiblichkeit!"* 291–94.

[47] See, for example, *Questions of Bartholomew* 2.8. I thank Ann Graham Brock
for this reference.

[48] Justin Martyr, *Dial.* 100.3–4; Irenaeus, *Haer.* 3.22.3–4; see Aloïs Müller,
Ecclesia—Mater: Die Einheit Marias und der Kirche (2d ed; Fribourg: Universitätsverlag, 1955); Amsler, *Acta Philippi: Commentarius,* 315–18. Actually
Hippolytus in his *Commentary on the Song of Songs* establishes a similar contrast, this time between Eve and the women at the empty tomb on the day of
Easter, particularly Mary Magdalene; see G. Nathanael Bonwetsch, *Hippolyts
Kommentar zum Hohenlied* 24–25 (TU 23/2; Leipzig: Hinrichs, 1902), 60–71. See
also in the *Acts of Andrew* 37(5) and 39(7) the pair Andrew-Maximilla reversing
the fate of Adam and Eve.

ministry.[49] Inscriptions from Asia Minor as well as council decisions (Council of Laodicea, canons 11 and 44) also mention or presuppose the presence of women ministers in the encratite communities.[50] We have here a new and strong confirmation.

What has not been noticed so far is the connection between women's ministry attested in *Acts Phil.* 1 and the ministerial activity of Mariamne described in *Acts Phil.* 8–*Mart.* At least for the compiler of the two parts in the fourth century C.E., but probably earlier already for the authors of *Acts Phil.* 1 and *Acts Phil.* 8–*Mart.*, Mariamne was not only a famous figure of the past. She was also the model and the justification for the present women's ministry. Those women who are called virgins, deaconesses, or priestesses could find an example to follow and to imitate in the figure of Mariamne. They have developed their manly faith and chosen the right type of clothing, not only a modest one, but also a masculine one. Virgins, deaconesses, and priestesses do not have the same function. The highest one, the priestess, must particularly feel a kinship with the apostle Mariamne as the priests identify themselves with the apostle Philip.

Such a daring spiritual ecclesiology combined with a dangerous Christology and an excessive ascetical life (to use the categories of the orthodox adversaries of the encratites of Asia Minor) explain why finally, despite its interest for the apostle Philip, a work like the *Acts of Philip* was rejected (its name is present on the list of the rejected books of the *Decretum gelasianum,* Gaul, sixth century C.E.). It is a miracle that nevertheless the manuscripts *Atheniensis 346* and the *Xenophontos 32* and to a lesser extent the *Vaticanus 824* have saved these stories from a complete shipwreck.[51]

---

[49] See Bertrand Bouvier and François Bovon, "Actes de Philippe, I, d'après un manuscrit inédit," in *Oecumenica et Patristica: Festschrift für Wilhelm Schneemelcher* (ed. D. Papandreou et al.; Geneva: Metropolie der Schweiz, 1989), 367–94, especially 393–94; Bovon, Bouvier, and Amsler, *Acta Philippi: Textus,* 29; Amsler, *Acta Philippi: Commentarius,* 81–82; Ute E. Eisen, *Women Officeholders in Early Christianity: Epigraphical and Literary Studies* (trans. L. M. Maloney; Collegeville, Minn.: Liturgical Press, 2000), 136. It escaped Karen Torjesen: see Karen Jo Torjesen, *When Women Were Priests: Women's Leadership in the Early Church and the Scandal of Their Subordination in the Rise of Christianity* (San Francisco: HarperSanFrancisco, 1993).

[50] See Amsler, *Acta Philippi: Commentarius,* 485–87; Eisen, *Women Officeholders in Early Christianity,* 116–23, 148–52.

[51] This paper was sent for publication when the following article was published: Stephen J. Shoemaker, "Rethinking the 'Gnostic Mary': Mary of Nazareth and Mary of Magdala in Early Christian Tradition," *JECS* 9 (2001): 555–95. I disagree with the author on several major points.

The Portrait of Mary in the *Ascension of Isaiah*

Jonathan Knight

Manchester Grammar School and University of Kent

It is reassuring to know that the topic of Mary continues to excite interest at the start of the third millennium. Whatever one's denominational affiliation, Mary remains a significant biblical character. She enjoyed a chequered career in biblical scholarship in the course of the twentieth century. Spurned by Protestants through faith in justification, she was "rediscovered" by an international committee of scholars (including Protestants) in 1978.[1] Since then Mary, like other biblical women,[2] has been the focus of interest, not least for feminist theologians.[3]

Mary's fate in scholarship is in many ways a test of progress and tolerance in the established denominations. No longer is it true to say that Protestants turn their backs on Mary because of the position she enjoys in Roman Catholic theology. Nor do Roman Catholics neglect the Bible when it comes to their evaluation of the mother of God. The time is ripe for the reconsideration of Mary's place in the contours of early Christian history and theology. This is what is being done, amongst other things, at this conference.

The adequacy of this broad assessment must be measured by its faithfulness to the early Christian texts. That means looking at *all* the available material, pseudepigraphal as well as canonical, and testing the foundations by collaborative exegesis of the relevant literature. That again is what is being done here. The opportunity to work in conjunction with other scholars is a welcome one indeed.

---

[1] Raymond E. Brown et al., eds., *Mary in the New Testament* (Philadelphia: Fortress; New York: Paulist, 1978).

[2] See J. Cheryl Exum, *Fragmented Women: Feminist (Sub)versions of Biblical Narratives* (JSOTSup 193; Sheffield: Sheffield Academic Press, 1993).

[3] See Rosemary Radford Ruether, *Mary: The Feminine Face of the Church* (Philadelphia: Westminster, 1977). See also Marina Warner, *Alone of All Her Sex: The Myth and Cult of the Virgin Mary* (London: Weidenfeld & Nicolson, 1976); Edward Schillebeeckx and Catharina Halkes, *Mary: Yesterday, Today, Tomorrow* (London: SCM, 1993); and John Macquarrie, *Mary for All Christians* (London: Collins, 1991).

This paper sets out to examine the portrait of Mary in the early Christian apocalypse known as the *Ascension of Isaiah*.[4] To do this requires several stages. First, we must examine the nature and date of this neglected text. Second, we must consider the question of what contact the *Ascension of Isaiah* has with Matthew's Gospel and with the traditions that lie behind Matthew. Only then can we consider the apocalypse itself. This examination of the *Ascension of Isaiah* must in turn be followed by the attempt to relate our findings to what is known about Mary from other ancient sources to assess the accuracy and value of the apocalypse for the study of this important topic.

1. The Text

When I first began working on the *Ascension of Isaiah* in the early 1980s, the volume of conference papers edited by Mauro Pesce had just appeared.[5] It is astonishing to note this was the first significant work on the apocalypse (with occasional exceptions) since R. H. Charles published his critical (and, in places, much criticized) edition of the text in 1900.[6] The past fifteen years have seen a resurgence of interest in the *Ascension of Isaiah*. This interest includes articles, books, and, above all, a reliable edition of the text in the Corpus Christianorum series apocryphorum produced by the Italian research team.[7] The time is now ripe to place the *Ascension of Isaiah*

---

[4] Critical edition by Paolo Bettiolo et al., eds., *Ascensio Isaiae: Textus* (CCSA 7; Turnhout: Brepols, 1995); commentary by Enrico Norelli, *Ascensio Isaiae: Commentarius* (CCSA 8; Turnhout: Brepols, 1995). The English translation cited in this paper is by Michael A. Knibb, "Martyrdom and Ascension of Isaiah," *OTP* 2:143–76.

[5] Mauro Pesce, ed., *Isaia, il Diletto e la chiesa: Visione ed esegesi profetica cristiano-primitiva nell'Ascensione di Isaia* (TRSR 20; Brescia: Paideia, 1983). Also from Italy come two books by Antonio Acerbi, *Serra lignea: Studi sulla fortuna della Ascensione di Isaia* (Rome: Editrice A.V.E., 1984); and *L'Ascensione di Isaia: Cristologia e profetismo in Siria nei primi decenni del II secolo* (SPMed 17; Milan: Vita e Pensiero, 1989); and two by Enrico Norelli, *L'Ascensione di Isaia: Studi su un apocrifo al crocevia dei cristianesimi* (Origini NS 1; Bologna: Dehoniane, 1994); and *Ascension du prophète Isaïe* (Apocryphes; Turnhout: Brepols, 1993).

[6] Robert H. Charles, *The Ascension of Isaiah* (London: Black, 1900).

[7] The new edition is detailed above. Among the articles, see Enrico Norelli, "Il martirio di Isaia come *testimonium* antigiudaico?" *Hen* 2 (1980): 37–56; idem, "La resurrezione di Gesù nell'*Ascensione di Isaia*," *CNS* 1 (1980): 315–66; Pier Cesare Bori, "L'estasi del profeta: 'Ascensio Isaiae' 6 e l'antico profetismo cristiano," *CNS* 1 (1980): 367–89; and Robert G. Hall, "The Ascension of Isaiah: Community Situation, Date, and Place in Early Christianity," *JBL* 109 (1990): 289–306; idem, "Isaiah's Ascent to See the Beloved: An Ancient Jewish Source for the Ascension of Isaiah," *JBL* 113 (1994): 463–84. Among the books, Robert G. Hall, *Revealed Histories: Techniques for Ancient Jewish Historiography* (JSPSup 6; Sheffield: Sheffield Academic Press,

under the microscope as was done at the beginning of the last century. I begin by asking the standard questions of what the *Ascension of Isaiah* is and when it was written.

The *Ascension of Isaiah* is a composite text that falls, rather obviously, into two halves. Charles assumed that the text was the work of a single hand or at least a single community. Yet Charles also proposed a complicated transmissional history for the work that the Italian team (in company with other scholars) now rejects.[8] In particular, they criticize the theory that a written *Martyrdom of Isaiah* was included in the work, preferring to think of the author's creative use of Jewish traditions but not of any written document as such. Norelli's view is that chapters 6–11 were written first and that chapters 1–5 were added by a different author, both stemming from the same circle of Christian prophets whose life and experiences the work reflects.[9] He thinks that chapters 6–11 were written at the end of the first century and that chapters 1–5 were added at the beginning of the second century.

This approach to the text contrasts with Charles's view that the work was finally compiled only at the end of the second or the beginning of the third century C.E. It accords with other recent work on the apocalypse. Relying on the possibility that *Ascen. Isa.* 4.13 alludes to the existence of living eyewitnesses of Jesus, Richard Bauckham dates the whole apocalypse to the decade 70 to 80 C.E.[10] In my own published work on the *Ascension of Isaiah* I have argued that the correspondence between Trajan and Pliny in the second decade of the second century is relevant exegetically. The possibility that the apocalypse stems from either the reign of Trajan or Hadrian seems to me a strong one. This means there is a reasonable consensus, against Charles, that the work comes from an early date, whether this is the period 70 to 80 C.E. or slightly later than that. This conclusion has the obvious corollary that the *Ascension of Isaiah* ranks among our earliest noncanonical Christian literature.

What, then, is the *Ascension of Isaiah,* and what does it reveal about this formative period of Christian history? The *Ascension of Isaiah* by common

---

1991), 137–47; and Jonathan Knight, *The Ascension of Isaiah* (Guides to Apocrypha and Pseudepigrapha 2; Sheffield: Sheffield Academic Press, 1995); idem, *Disciples of the Beloved One: The Christology, Social Setting and Theological Context of the Ascension of Isaiah* (JSPSup 18; Sheffield: Sheffield Academic Press, 1996).

8 See especially M. Pesce, "Presupposti per l'utilizzazione storica dell'*Ascensione di Isaia:* Formazione e tradizione del testo, genere letterario, cosmologia angelica," in Pesce, *Isaia,* 13–76.

9 In his *Ascensio Isaiae: Commentarius.*

10 "The Ascension of Isaiah: Genre, Unity and Date," in his *The Fate of the Dead: Studies on the Jewish and Christian Apocalypses* (Leiden: Brill, 1998), 363–90.

consent is an apocalypse. That is to say, it is a revelatory work with a narrative introduction in which heavenly secrets are disclosed to provide assurance of eschatological salvation. Interestingly, the *Ascension of Isaiah* falls into both the categories discerned in the 1979 Collins morphology of the apocalypse genre.[11] Chapters 1–5 disclose futurist eschatology but lack a heavenly journey. Chapters 6–11 include a heavenly journey but do not say a great deal about futurist eschatology. While we should not rush to conclude that this difference means the two halves of the apocalypse come from different authors, the differences between them must not be minimized.

I do not feel it necessary (for which my readers may even thank me) to engage in a detailed discussion of the "ins and outs" of a particular literary-critical view of the *Ascension of Isaiah*. I shall content myself with observing the different opinions that have been held and offer a short, and I hope succinct, introduction to the contents of the apocalypse.

The form of chapters 1–5 is strongly reminiscent of the book of Daniel.[12] There is a narrative introduction. This describes the misfortune that occurred when Manasseh acceded to the Judean throne. The essential theme of this narrative is that Manasseh is a lawless king dominated by the supernatural adversary whom the text calls variously Beliar, Sammael, Malkira, and Satan. Manasseh persecutes those who remain faithful to their ancestral religion. Isaiah and his friends withdraw to the desert and found a community there. It is said of them that "all of them were clothed in sackcloth, and all of them were prophets; they had nothing with them, but were destitute, and they all lamented bitterly over the going astray of Israel" (*Ascen. Isa.* 2.10). At the beginning of chapter 3, Isaiah and community are harassed in their retreat by the false prophet Belkira. Belkira denounces them before Manasseh on a series of charges (evidently false ones). Isaiah is arrested and brought before Manasseh (*Ascen. Isa.* 3.12).

This is the introduction to the first revelatory section of the work. In form, this is a historical review that divides history (as does Daniel) into different representative periods.[13] The first period is the life of Jesus, which is presented in terms of the descent and ascension of a divine being between heaven and earth (*Ascen. Isa.* 3.13–18). The second period is the apostolic age (*Ascen. Isa.* 3.19–20). This is described as a period inspired by the Holy Spirit and characterized by "many signs and miracles" (*Ascen. Isa.* 3.20). There is a marked sea-change in *Ascen. Isa.* 3.21–31. This is the

[11] John J. Collins, ed., *Apocalypse: The Morphology of a Genre* (*Semeia* 14; Missoula, Mont.: Scholars Press, 1979).

[12] This point is made by Bauckham, "The Ascension of Isaiah."

[13] See Hall, *Revealed Histories,* 137–47.

third historical period, in which it is evident that the author himself lives. The author complains that the voice of prophecy is being repressed and that "many wicked elders and shepherds ... wrong their sheep" (*Ascen. Isa.* 3.24). *Ascension of Isaiah* 3.31 apparently mentions an attempt to silence the author himself.

The construction of this historical review is probably suggested by the Danielic precedent, most obviously by Dan 10–12. There is a shift from present to future reporting at the beginning of chapter 4, much as *Ascen. Isa.* 3.21 witnessed the shift from past to present reporting. Two traditions are fused together in *Ascen. Isa.* 4.1–13 to predict that the demon Beliar will incarnate himself in the person of Nero *redivivus*. The suggestion is that only a faithful remnant of Christians will be left as a result of this appearance (*Ascen. Isa.* 4.13). The remedy for this assault is prescribed by *Ascen. Isa.* 4.14–18. This section predicts that "the Lord will come with his angels and with the hosts of the saints from the seventh heaven, with the glory of the seventh heaven, and will drag Beliar, and his hosts also, into Gehenna" (*Ascen. Isa.* 4.14). The world will then be destroyed and the righteous ascend with their redeemer to enjoy a form of immortality in the heavenly world. Chapter 5 is a narrative conclusion to the first half of the work. It describes how Isaiah was executed by Manasseh for his visionary predictions, attributing this repression to demonic interference.

Chapters 6–11 are markedly different in character. They narrate a mystical ascension in which Isaiah journeys to the seventh heaven to witness the saving action of the descending redeemer.[14] Although both the preparations for the ascension (ch. 6) and the descent through the lower heavens (chs. 7 and 8) are described in some detail, it is clear that the author's real interest lies in the mediator's descent, which is narrated in chapters 9 and 10. It lies beyond the purpose of a paper on Mary to explain the problems of this section in detail. I will say only that the death of Jesus on the cross has the effect of pronouncing the fate of the demonic powers in anticipation of their final destruction at the Parousia so that in fact there is a link between the two halves of the work in terms of their eschatological understanding. The Christology can be compared to a parabola in which the redeemer descends from the seventh heaven, appears on earth as Jesus,

---

14 This motif was studied classically by Wilhelm Bousset, *Die Himmelsreise der Seele* (1901; repr., Darmstadt: Wissenschaftliche Buchgesellschaft, 1971). Among the recent literature, see Martha Himmelfarb, *Ascent to Heaven in Jewish and Christian Apocalypses* (Oxford: Oxford University Press, 1993); and Adela Yarbro Collins, *Cosmology and Eschatology in Jewish and Christian Apocalypticism* (Leiden: Brill, 1996).

and returns to the seventh heaven. There are significant parallels to this form of belief in Jewish angelology.[15]

The major problem chapters 6–11 throw up is the presence of some traditions about Jesus in chapter 11.[16] This is a convenient cue to look back to chapter 3. *Ascension of Isaiah* 3.13–18 also contains some traditions about Jesus whose origin and affinities we shall consider in a moment. Nothing is said there about Mary. Mary, however, features strongly in the parallel traditions in chapter 11. The problem with chapter 11 is that these traditions are found in only one branch of the textual tradition, that represented by the Ethiopic translation (E). The Slavonic and one of the two Latin translations (S and L2) replace them with a short summary of the earthly appearance so that their authenticity—including the Marian material—is disputed.

This is a difficult problem for all serious study of the *Ascension of Isaiah*. Two factors suggest that we are dealing with material that is germane to the *Ascension of Isaiah* and not with a later insertion in chapter 11. On the consensus understanding of the apocalypse, the two halves come from identical or closely related authors.[17] In fact, it is more important to demonstrate the common outlook of the two halves of the *Ascension of Isaiah* than to insist on common authorship throughout. This common outlook is confirmed by the presence of such distinctive ideas as the notion of the seven heavens, the demonology, and, above all, by the title "Beloved One" used for the descending redeemer. It is hardly coincidence that these occur in both halves of the *Ascension of Isaiah,* distinguishing the apocalypse in this respect from all other early Christian literature. The *Ascension of Isaiah* coheres in its present form, whatever the *precise* circumstances of its literary composition.

The presence of the Jesus traditions in chapter 3 makes them difficult to remove from chapter 11. Whilst the Jesus traditions in the two chapters are different in content, they fulfill an identical purpose in the text. They describe the life of Jesus within the wider context of the myth of the descending-ascending redeemer. (This is particularly true if Norelli is right to suggest that chapters 6–11 were composed subsequently to the first half of the *Ascension of Isaiah*.) This mythology is obvious in chapter 11, where the story of Jesus is preceded by the description of how the mediator descended through the heavens in response to his divine commission (ch. 10). It is no less obvious in *Ascen. Isa.* 3.13, where the Jesus traditions are introduced with the words, "that through [Isaiah] there had been revealed

---

[15] See my *Disciples,* ch. 2.

[16] See my review of this issue in ibid., 26–27.

[17] So, recently, Bauckham, "The Ascension of Isaiah."

the coming of the Beloved from the seventh heaven, and his transformation, and his descent, and the form into which he must be transformed, (namely) the form of a man." This common outlook argues strongly that *Ascen. Isa.* 11.2–22 in the Ethiopic text is an original part of the *Ascension of Isaiah* and not a later insertion.

This conclusion is supported by a second consideration. *Ascension of Isaiah* 11.2–22 seems to make concessions in a docetic direction, or at least it can be read in that way. It is possible that a later editor found this section either too docetic or possibly insufficiently docetic and removed it for that reason. It is very substantially easier to see *Ascen. Isa.* 11.2–22, with all its warts, as part of the original apocalypse than to treat it as later hagiography. In doing this, we must take due account of the mythological context in which this material occurs.

2. *The Jesus Traditions in the* Ascension of Isaiah

The next question to consider is the origin of these Jesus traditions, including the question of whether they have contact with New Testament descriptions of Jesus and Mary.

The Jesus traditions have an inner coherence that suggests they were not created *de novo* by the author(s) of the *Ascension of Isaiah*. This view has been carefully argued by Richard Bauckham.[18] Bauckham compares these "kerygmatic summaries" (as he calls them) with the summaries included in Acts and then again in Ignatius of Antioch and elsewhere. There are three such summaries in the *Ascension of Isaiah*. Besides *Ascen. Isa.* 3.13–18 and 11.2–22 (E), already mentioned, we must notice *Ascen. Isa.* 9.13–18, where it is said of the mediator's earthly appearance that "the LORD will indeed descend into the world in the last days, (he) who is to be called Christ after he has descended and become like you in form, and they will think that he is flesh and a man." This is followed in chapter 9 by a prediction of the death and the resurrection of Jesus.

These summaries are not plain narrative descriptions of Jesus. They have a mythological quality in the sense that they describe the appearance of a divine being in the world who dies because he is unrecognized there but rises and ascends back to his exalted position in the seventh heaven. Bauckham identifies verbal points of contact with the other "kerygmatic summaries" mentioned. These reinforce the conclusion that they belong to this particular genre and are not simply individual abstractions made on the basis of the Gospels. Thus the phrase "signs and wonders" (*Ascen. Isa.* 11.18) occurs in

---

[18] "Kerygmatic Summaries in the Speeches of Acts," in *History, Literature and Society in the Book of Acts* (ed. Ben Witherington; Cambridge: Cambridge University Press, 1996), 185–217, esp. 191–204.

both Acts 2:22 and *T. Adam* 3.1 but in the Gospels only derogatorily in John 4:48; and the "punishments with which the children of Israel must punish him" occurs in a fragment of the *Kerygma Petrou* preserved in Clement of Alexandria *Strom.* 6.15.128 but not in the New Testament.

The essence of the "kerygmatic summary," against Martin Dibelius,[19] was its flexibility as an organ of communication in earliest Christianity. In this, it contrasts with the fixed form of the Gospels, especially as the first century went through its course. The variation both in style and in content between the summaries in different works suggests there was a common stock of such material in Christian antiquity from which individual units were composed.

The *Ascension of Isaiah* appears to be a unique work in a number of important respects, the summaries included. One such respect is the idiosyncratic fusion of the "kerygmatic summary" material with the myth of the descending-ascending redeemer in the apocalypse. This was the work of the author himself. It is not necessary to suppose that he derived the mythological element from the "kerygmatic summary" tradition. It was an emerging feature of late first-century Christianity, as we know from the Fourth Gospel (and possibly even earlier, depending on the evaluation of Phil 2:5–11). As with other aspects of his apocalypse, this author shows a creative use of existing material that combines ideas to present them in a new and arresting way.

We must ask how these "kerygmatic summaries" in the *Ascension of Isaiah* relate to the crystallizing Gospel tradition of the New Testament. Even a casual reading of the apocalypse shows that these traditions have contact with Matthew's Gospel in particular. Thus *Ascen. Isa.* 3.13 blames the "children of Israel" for the suffering of Jesus (see the narrative of Matt 27, esp. Matt 27:25); *Ascen. Isa.* 3.14 mentions the guards at the tomb (see Matt 27:62–66; 28:11–15); *Ascen. Isa.* 3.15 mentions the descent of an angel to effect the resurrection (see Matt 28:2); *Ascen. Isa.* 3.18 makes the disciples "teach all nations and every tongue the resurrection of the Beloved" (see Matt 28:19); and *Ascen. Isa.* 11.2–7 tells the story of the conception and birth of Jesus in language that has obvious parallels with Matt 1:18–25.

This relationship with Matthew has been variously evaluated in recent scholarship. Bauckham assigns the material to the "kerygmatic summary" tradition and thus distinguishes it from Matthew itself. He is followed in this by Norelli in more than one publication.[20] E. Massaux, on the other

---

[19] *From Tradition to Gospel* (London: Nicholson & Watson, 1934), 16–17.

[20] *L'Ascensione di Isaia,* 115–66, esp. 116–42; "Avant le canonique et l'apocryphe: aux origines des récits de la naissance de Jésus," *RTP* 126 (1994): 305–24; *Ascensio Isaiae: Commentarius,* ch. 1 paragraph 8.

hand, notes special affinities with Matthew in *Ascen. Isa.* 3.17–18a and finds even the possible reminiscence of Matthew in *Ascen. Isa.* 3.18a.[21] W.-D. Köhler holds more than one passage influenced by Matthew.[22] This argument was more recently restated by J. Verheyden, who discerns three elements indicating our author's dependence on Matthew: the guard at the tomb, the descent of the angel, and the mission of the disciples.[23] A *via media* is the hypothesis of B. A. Johnson and J. Denker that there was a tradition common to both Matthew and the *Gospel of Peter* of which the *Ascension of Isaiah* is a third representative.[24]

It will be helpful to clarify the issues involved in this discussion. First of all, the *Ascension of Isaiah* is an apocalypse and not a Gospel. Secondly, the *Ascension of Isaiah* includes no substantial citations from Matthew that would put the question of Matthean influence beyond possible doubt. Thirdly, there is most certainly a connection between the *Ascension of Isaiah* and Matthew's *special material*. Fourthly, however, this connection does not necessarily mean that the author used Matthew itself. He could have drawn on the source that provided Matthew's special material so that it is not proven to posit direct literary dependence in explanation of the facts in question. The latter argument is accepted as convincing by Norelli in particular.

Were Bauckham's argument about the date of the *Ascension of Isaiah* to be accepted, that would place the issue beyond doubt. The author of the apocalypse cannot have known a text that was not yet written or only just written. Even if the *Ascension of Isaiah* comes from the early second century, however, the hypothesis that the author drew on Matthew itself faces two considerable objections: (1) nothing in *Ascen. Isa.* 11.2–22 necessarily demands dependence on the text of Matthew as opposed to a common source; and (2) both the strange description of the resurrection in *Ascen. Isa.* 3.16–17 (see *Gos. Pet.* 34–42) and the statement about the absent

---

[21] Edouard Massaux, *Influence de l'évangile de saint Matthieu sur la littérature chrétienne avant saint Irénée* (BETL 75; reissued, Leuven: Leuven University Press, 1986), 196.

[22] *Die Rezeption des Matthäusevangeliums in der Zeit vor Irenäus* (WUNT 24; Tübingen: Mohr Siebeck, 1987), 303, 307.

[23] "L'Ascension d'Isaïe et Matthieu," in *The New Testament in Early Christianity: La réception des écrits néotestamentaires dans le christianisme primitif* (ed. J.-M. Sevrin; BETL 86; Leuven: Leuven University Press, 1989), 247–74.

[24] B. A. Johnson, "The Gospel of Peter: Between Apocalypse and Romance," in *StPatr* 16 (TU 129; Berlin: de Gruyter, 1985), 2:170–74; Jürgen Denker, *Die theologiegeschichtliche Stellung des Petrusevangeliums: Ein Beitrag zur Frühgeschichte des Doketismus* (Europaische Hochschulschriften: Theologie 36; Bern: Lang, 1975), 151.

midwife in *Ascen. Isa.* 11.14, which have no Matthean parallels, point in favor of the common source theory.

My conclusion, in which I follow Norelli, is thus that the evidence of *Ascen. Isa.* 11.2–22 in the Ethiopic version suggests the author used a pre-Matthean source for the summaries that Matthew also utilized. This is an important conclusion for studying the Marian traditions in the apocalypse. It shows that, even if chapters 6–11 come from the second century C.E., they incorporate earlier material so that we are placed in touch with traditions about Jesus that circulated in the first century C.E., evidently before the writing of the canonical gospels.

3. Mary in the Ascension of Isaiah

Now for the real content of this paper. What does the *Ascension of Isaiah* say about Mary, and how does this information cohere with what is known about Mary from elsewhere?

The Marian traditions in the *Ascension of Isaiah* are confined to the disputed passage in the Ethiopic text of chapter 11, which I have held an authentic part of the apocalypse (*Ascen. Isa.* 11.2–22 E). I shall begin by listing what the apocalypse says about Mary and then proceed to the issue of interpretation.

Ascension of Isaiah 11.2 states that Mary was "a woman of the family of David" and that she was betrothed to Joseph the carpenter who was also a Davidide. *Ascension of Isaiah* 11.3 continues that Mary was found pregnant and that Joseph resolved to divorce her. In *Ascen. Isa.* 11.4 "the angel of the Spirit appeared in this world," and Joseph gave up his plan. According to *Ascen. Isa.* 11.5–6 Joseph kept Mary a virgin and did not live with her for two months. After this time (*Ascen. Isa.* 11.8) "Mary then looked with her eyes and saw a small infant, and she was astounded." *Ascension of Isaiah* 11.9 adds that "after her astonishment had worn off, her womb was found as (it was) at first, before she had conceived." *Ascension of Isaiah* 11.12–13 records popular mystification about the birth of Jesus, some saying that Mary had given birth after only two months but others that she did not give birth because no midwife had attended her. This part of the summary ends with the words, strikingly similar to Ignatius, *Eph.* 19, "it was hidden from all the heavens and all the princes and every god of this world" (*Ascen. Isa.* 11.16).

The first statement (*Ascen. Isa.* 11.2) supplies more information about Mary than does Matthew.[25] Matthew 1 makes Joseph a Davidide, tracing Jesus' ancestry on the paternal side. Luke 1:27 also makes Joseph a

---

[25] For exegesis of the canonical material, see Raymond E. Brown, *The Birth of the Messiah* (2 vols.; New York: Doubleday, 1993).

Davidide, but, although the attempt to do this was occasionally made in the patristic period, it does not seem likely that this reference includes Mary. Indeed, Luke introduces a complication on this very point. He gives Mary Levitical relatives as if she came from a different tribe altogether. The *Ascension of Isaiah* must be compared with such second-century sources as *Prot. Jas.* 10.1; Ignatius, *Eph.* 18.2; and Justin, *Dial.* 44.4, in making Mary a Davidide. The fact that this information is found in second-century sources but not in first-century sources almost certainly makes it suspect historically. The only safe conclusion is that these sources are "improving" what was known about Joseph's ancestry to include Mary in order to remove any possible doubt about Jesus' messianic qualifications. Like Luke's attribution of priestly ancestry to Mary, it is possible—if not probable—that theological motivations have entered the arena at this point. (There is no evidence that the author of the *Ascension of Isaiah* knew the text of Luke.)

The next section of the "kerygmatic summary" (*Ascen. Isa.* 11.3–6) closely resembles the account in Matt 1:18–21. Although the language used is peculiar to the *Ascension of Isaiah,* the thought is the same as Matthew's. This is that Joseph was dissuaded from divorcing Mary through an angelophany and that he had no sexual relations with her before the birth of Jesus. The *Ascension of Isaiah* leaves no doubt about the virginal conception of Jesus but makes no attempt to explain how this occurred except by implying the "angel of the Spirit's" role in this matter.

By contrast, the description of the birth of Jesus is strikingly different from Matthew's account. It seems on the basis of *Ascen. Isa.* 11.8 (E) that Mary gave birth to Jesus after a pregnancy of only two months. The birth itself took the mother by surprise. The implication is that it occurred in Bethlehem, based on the statement that Joseph was a Davidide (*Ascen. Isa.* 11.2), the reference to Joseph's house (*Ascen. Isa.* 11.7), and the subsequent journey to Nazareth (*Ascen. Isa.* 11.15). Of greater interest than the location is the manner of the birth in question. Mary's pregnancy is said to have lasted for two months only. It is not easy to explain the origin of this figure, except perhaps to dispute the possibility that it came from the tradition held in common with Matthew. *Protevangelium of James* 13.1 states that Mary gave birth in the sixth month of her pregnancy. Of the Evangelists, only Luke takes an interest in the duration of Mary's pregnancy (Luke 1:26, 56).

It is probable that, in evaluating this material, we should focus less on the specific duration of the pregnancy than on the supernatural nature of the event as indicated by its brevity. The short pregnancy must be related to the notion of the mediator's descent from heaven and the other indications of his superhuman ability in *Ascen. Isa.* 11.2–22, including the implied suggestion that Jesus did not really *need* to suck the breast in *Ascen. Isa.* 11.17 and his "signs and miracles," which are reported in *Ascen. Isa.* 11.18.

It places beyond any possible doubt the divine hand in the events and states, in chronological terms, the author's conviction that this baby was no ordinary human being. The *Ascension of Isaiah* and the *Protevangelium of James* represent different variations on this theme.

The birth of Jesus in the *Ascension of Isaiah* is apparently a spontaneous event. Again, this must be referred to the author's superimposition of the mythological pattern. The point is that a heavenly visitor needs no human assistance when incarnating himself on earth. The thought is that the Beloved One passes through Mary's womb, although the pregnancy and birth are real events. The infant does not bypass Mary's womb in appearing from heaven. This information must be compared with the other exceptional deeds of Jesus recorded in *Ascen. Isa.* 11.17–18. It is a Christology, not an early Marian adulation.

The final point is historically the most significant. We saw that, in *Ascen. Isa.* 11.9 (E), "after her astonishment had worn off, her womb was found as (it was) at first, before she had conceived." This is the middle term in the fourth-century triad, *ante partum, in partu,* and *post partum*.[26] Here the *Ascension of Isaiah* differs from Matthew and Luke, which, in that order, state or imply that Jesus was virginally conceived. The *Ascension of Isaiah* not only states that Jesus was virginally conceived but adds that Mary was found a virgin following the delivery. Once again, one wonders whether this element was introduced by the author of the *Ascension of Isaiah* rather than derived from the tradition held in common with Matthew. The point at stake is the confirmation that Jesus was not conceived by human means. In the context of the author's Christology, this is because he is the Beloved One who had descended from the seventh heaven. This evidence should be compared with that of *Prot. Jas.* 19–20, where it is said, somewhat graphically, that the hymen was not ruptured during the delivery of Jesus.

The overriding impression to emerge from this material is that the birth of Jesus, like his conception, was a miracle. That is why no midwife attended (*Ascen. Isa.* 11.14). This was no ordinary baby. The progress of thought in the summary is from the birth to the adulthood of Jesus. The material is set within the context of the wider mythological pattern that describes the action of the descending and ascending redeemer. That is the context in which the Marian material must be interpreted.

4. Evaluation of the Material

The final question to address is how we evaluate this material and what contact it demonstrates with other Christian literature describing the birth of Jesus.

---

[26] See ibid., 517–33.

We have seen that there is both contact with Matthew's Gospel and also obvious differences from Matthew. In places, it is difficult to avoid the conclusion that these differences are deliberate and theologically nuanced. The principal differences I have noticed are twofold. First of all, the birth of Jesus is a spontaneous event that escapes even the mother's notice. Secondly, Mary is found a virgin after the delivery. Both of these are christological statements. They reflect the belief that Jesus is the earthly appearance of the Beloved One, the divine mediator who came from the seventh heaven. In both cases, I questioned whether it is plausible to suppose that the author derived them from the tradition held in common with Matthew.

With due allowance to the recognition that ideas do not develop in a strict chronological sequence, I want to place this difference-within-similarity in a trajectory and examine the relation between Matthew and the *Ascension of Isaiah* in that perspective. Matthew itself lives within a trajectory when compared with Mark. Matthew introduced the infancy narrative over against Mark as if to make the point that Jesus was the Messiah from even before his birth. It is plausible to see Luke as to some extent revising Matthew and then to see John as reading back the significance of Jesus to the moment of creation itself. This trajectory within the Gospels cannot be ignored when writing on the Christology of the New Testament literature.

Matthew introduces the idea of Jesus' virginal conception apparently for the purpose of demonstrating that Isa 7:14 has been fulfilled (Matt 1:22–23). The silence of the earlier New Testament writings about the virginal conception is certainly significant theologically, and it may be significant historically. Luke tones down the idea of virginal conception, removing the scriptural "proof" and allowing the reader to *infer* it from his text (Luke 1:34–35). It is not the purpose of this paper to ask why Matthew introduces this idea, but the question is a pertinent one for all study of Mary in early Christian literature. The *Ascension of Isaiah* offers a parallel version to Matthew's, making additions that reinforce the virginal conception whilst omitting the scriptural proof for it. The latter suggests that the scriptural proof is a Matthean innovation.

Cui bono? is a familiar phrase to New Testament scholars. In the present context we must ask to whose advantage these additions are made: to Jesus' or to Mary's. It has occasionally been suggested that the *Ascension of Isaiah* is an early witness to the developing cult of Mary.[27] I want to resist that suggestion here. The passage where the information occurs is

---

[27] See F. Buck, "Are the 'Ascension of Isaiah' and the 'Odes of Solomon' Witnesses to an Early Cult of Mary?" in *De primordiis cultus mariani* (Rome: Pontificia academia mariana internationalis, 1970), 4:371–99.

one of three "kerygmatic summaries" in the *Ascension of Isaiah* and the only one where she is mentioned. Moreover, the additions point ultimately beyond Mary to the figure of the Beloved One who passed with such ease through her womb. Nor is there any attempt to describe the miraculous conception of Mary herself, as there is for instance in the *Protevangelium of James*. Significantly also, there is no suggestion of the *virginitas post partum;* the *Ascension of Isaiah* does nothing to contradict the statement of the Gospels that Jesus had brothers and sisters, even though it does not specifically mention it.[28]

In terms of my proposed trajectory, however rough it may be, the *Ascension of Isaiah* represents a development beyond Matthew in certain respects but not so far as the *Protevangelium of James*. As opposed to Matthew, Jesus' parents form an element in the kerygmatic summary, not its basic framework. The framework is provided by the myth of the descending-ascending redeemer. That determines the form of the material utilized. The miraculous birth of Jesus and its lack of human involvement point to the influence of the heavenly world, not to the human circumstances of the mediator's earthly appearance. The summary concludes as it began with a heavenly journey, in this case, the ascent of the Beloved through the seven heavens (*Ascen. Isa.* 11.23–33). Mary features as an actor in the summary, not the central character. The "descent-ascent" scheme provides the framework into which the Marian traditions are inserted in this apocalypse.

The use of Marian traditions in the apocalypse is christologically determined. What is said about Mary supports the miraculous nature of the intervention that the heavenly descent scheme introduces. The *Ascension of Isaiah* both augments the notion of the virginal conception and makes the birth of Jesus take his mother by surprise. This leaves no doubt that Jesus' person and ministry are conceived in supernatural terms. It is interesting to ponder the question of whether there is a "crypto-docetism" in the *Ascension of Isaiah* that was introduced to support this view.[29]

We can but ponder the source of the *virginitas in partu*. Given that the *Ascension of Isaiah* is earlier than the *Protevangelium of James,* it is possible—but not certain—that the author was himself responsible for the creation of this idea. In any event the *Ascension of Isaiah* illustrates the way in which Marian ideas were developing around the end of the first century C.E. It shows that christological interest in no small measure prompted this early flowering.

---

[28] On whom see Richard J. Bauckham, *Jude and the Relatives of Jesus in the Early Church* (Edinburgh: T&T Clark, 1990).

[29] On this subject, see now Darrell D. Hannah, "Isaiah's Vision in the Ascension of Isaiah and the Early Church," *JTS* 50 (1999): 80–101.

The significance of the *Ascension of Isaiah* for our topic lies in its early date and the differences that emerge when it is compared with Matthew. The most likely explanation of this difference is that both authors used common tradition in different ways. We must also contrast the view of Mary in the *Ascension of Isaiah* with the much more developed hagiography of the *Protevangelium of James*. When this is done, and to introduce a crude historical anachronism, I venture to suggest that the *Ascension of Isaiah* has more in common with the beliefs of the later first century than it does with the beliefs of the later second century. The apocalypse lets us "take a level" on Marian belief at the time when the canonical gospels were just about finished. The *Ascension of Isaiah* thereby stands as historical commentary of the very highest importance. In its Marian traditions it goes beyond the *virginitas ante partum,* but it does not yet reach the level of apocryphal Marian hagiography that later texts introduce. It confirms the continuing importance of the pre-Gospel tradition and illustrates the use that was made of such material during the period in question.

Seeking the Source of the Marian Myth: Have We Found the Missing Link?[1]

George T. Zervos
The University of North Carolina at Wilmington

Two early pseudepigraphical documents afford us the opportunity to peer into the murky world of early Christian traditions concerning Mary, the mother of Jesus. One of these, the *Protevangelium of James,* is a New Testament apocryphon whose primary concern is the person of Mary. The other document, the *Ascension of Isaiah,* is commonly categorized as an Old Testament pseudepigraphon,[2] although it contains at least some manifestly Christian material.[3] *Ascension of Isaiah* 11.2–16 constitutes an important witness to early Christian traditions about Mary apart from those commonly known from the canonical gospels. These include Mary's Davidic descent, her astonishment at the miraculous appearance of the infant Jesus after a short two-month pregnancy, the absence of a midwife in the nativity, and Mary's *virginitas post partum.* Both the *Ascension of Isaiah* and the *Protevangelium of James* have suffered from decades of neglect by scholars, with the result that their significance for the study of the origin and early development of Christian, and especially Marian, traditions has been seriously underestimated.

The paucity of original critical investigation of the *Protevangelium of James* has resulted in the entrenchment and perpetuation of an older scholarly consensus of opinion with regard to its date and compositional character[4]

---

[1] This article was prepared as a response to "The Portrait of Mary in the *Ascension of Isaiah,*" a paper read by Jonathan Knight to the Christian Apocrypha Section at the Annual Meeting of the AAR/SBL in Nashville, Tennessee, in November, 2000.

[2] The *Ascension of Isaiah* is included in such classic collections of Old Testament pseudepigrapha as Robert H. Charles, *The Apocrypha and Pseudepigrapha of the Old Testament* (2 vols.; Oxford: Oxford University Press, 1913), 2:155–62; and *OTP* 2:156–76.

[3] *Ascen. Isa.* 3.13–4.22; 9.13–18; 11.2–22.

[4] George T. Zervos, "Dating the Protevangelium of James: The Justin Martyr Connection," *SBL Seminar Papers, 1994* (SBLSP 33; Atlanta: Scholars Press, 1994), 415–34.

that has effectively neutralized the perceived importance of this document for the study of early Christian thought. Hence the *Protevangelium of James* has been relegated to an inglorious position as a secondary writing of the middle to late second century C.E. with little or no presumable relevance for the study of earliest Christianity.[5] It is a difficult task to overcome the inertia of a well-entrenched scholarly consensus and to argue in favor of an earlier date—and therefore enhanced significance—for a noncanonical document vis-à-vis its canonical and, in this case, noncanonical counterparts. This writer has been a φωνὴ βοῶντος ἐν τῇ ἐρήμῳ in just such a process for the past two decades with regard to the *Protevangelium of James*.[6] In the present paper I will support the position that the *Protevangelium of James* (or one of its source documents), which has been ignored as a factor in the critical assessment of the Marian traditions in the *Ascension of Isaiah*, could constitute the "missing link" that may hold the answers to some of the questions posed by the advanced Mariology of the *Ascension of Isaiah*.

In contrast to the *Protevangelium of James,* the *Ascension of Isaiah* has succeeded in gaining the esteem of the scholarly world. This is due largely to the efforts of what is referred to as "the Italian team," a group of Italian researchers who have studied the *Ascension of Isaiah* intensively during the last twenty years and have produced a number of seminal publications pertaining to this document.[7] Nevertheless, recognition and acceptance of the work of the Italian team by scholars has been painfully slow. As recently as 1996 Richard Bauckham described as "scandalous" the disregard for the early publications of the Italian researchers by recent major reference works in their treatments of the *Ascension of Isaiah*.[8] However, the most recent

---

[5] Ibid., 415–18.

[6] George T. Zervos, "Prolegomena to a Critical Edition of the *Genesis Marias* (*Protevangelium Jacobi*): The Greek Manuscripts" (Ph.D. diss., Duke University, 1986); idem, "Dating"; idem, "An Early Non-canonical Annunciation Story," *SBL Seminar Papers, 1997* (SBLSP 36; Atlanta: Scholars Press, 1997), 664–91.

[7] These include a comprehensive critical edition of the text of the *Ascension of Isaiah*, Paolo Bettiolo et al., eds., *Ascensio Isaiae: Textus* (CCSA 7; Turnhout: Brepols, 1995), with accompanying exhaustive commentary by the foremost of the team, Enrico Norelli, *Ascensio Isaiae: Commentarius* (CCSA 8; Turnhout: Brepols, 1995). For a brief but thorough survey of the Italian scholars and their publications, see Richard Bauckham, "The Ascension of Isaiah: Genre, Unity, and Date," in his *The Fate of the Dead: Studies on the Jewish and Christian Apocalypses* (NovTSup 93; Leiden: Brill, 1998), 363–65.

[8] "Kerygmatic Summaries in the Speeches of Acts," in *History, Literature, and Society in the Book of Acts* (ed. B. Witherington; Cambridge: Cambridge University Press, 1996), 191 n. 19; idem, "Ascension," 364–65; Jonathan Knight, *Disciples of the*

scholarly investigations of the *Ascension of Isaiah*[9] have taken full account of the monumental work of the "Italian team." This has resulted in a complete reassessment of the critical issues surrounding this pseudepigraphon.

Whereas previous researchers viewed the *Ascension of Isaiah* as a composite work made up of earlier source documents that were joined together by a later editor,[10] the latest trend among scholars has been to emphasize the unity of the *Ascension of Isaiah* as a whole and especially that of chapters 6–11.[11] The *Ascension of Isaiah* is now considered to be an early second-century Christian apocalypse made up of two parts: chapters 1–5, containing a narrative introduction to the whole work and disclosures of futuristic eschatology, and chapters 6–11, describing Isaiah's mystical journey to the seventh heaven, where he witnesses the descent, earthly sojourn, and ascent of the heavenly redeemer followed by a narrative conclusion to the whole document. The final chapter of this second, and some think older,[12] section of the *Ascension of Isaiah* narrates the birth of the Lord Christ by Mary (including the important Marian witness in *Ascen. Isa.* 11.2–16), his infancy, life, crucifixion, resurrection, and ascension again to the seventh heaven, where he takes his place at the right hand of the "Great Glory."

The newly acquired scholarly respect for the *Ascension of Isaiah* necessitates a reassessment of the significance of the advanced Marian

---

Beloved One: The Christology, Social Setting and Theological Context of the Ascension of Isaiah (JSPSup 18; Sheffield: Sheffield Academic Press, 1996), 5, 13.

[9] Bauckham, "Ascension," 363–91; Darrell D. Hannah, "Isaiah's Vision in the Ascension of Isaiah and the Early Church," *JTS* 50 (1999): 80–101; Loren T. Stuckenbruck, "Worship and Monotheism in the Ascension of Isaiah," in *The Jewish Roots of Christological Monotheism: Papers from the St. Andrews Conference on the Historical Origins of the Worship of Jesus* (ed. C. C. Newman et al.; JSJSup 63; Leiden: Brill, 1999), 70–89.

[10] Robert H. Charles, *The Ascension of Isaiah* (London: Black, 1900); Michael A. Knibb, "Martyrdom and Ascension of Isaiah," *OTP* 2:143–55.

[11] Jonathan Knight, *The Ascension of Isaiah* (Guides to Apocrypha and Pseudepigrapha 2; Sheffield: Sheffield Academic Press, 1995); idem, *Disciples,* 28–32; Bauckham, "Summaries," 191–92; and especially idem, "Ascension," 365–80, where Bauckham presents an overview of scholarly opinions on the composition of the *Ascension of Isaiah* and his own detailed response to the theory of Norelli, *Ascensio Isaiae: Commentarius,* 36–52; Robert G. Hall, "Isaiah's Ascent to See the Beloved: An Ancient Jewish Source for the Ascension of Isaiah?" *JBL* 113 (1994): 463–84, in contrast to his earlier work, "The Ascension of Isaiah: Community Situation, Date, and Place in Early Christianity," *JBL* 109 (1990): 289–306; Hannah, "Vision," 84–85; Stuckenbruck, "Worship," 70–71 nn. 1, 2.

[12] See discussion with references in Bauckham, "Ascension," 365–71.

traditions presented in *Ascen. Isa.* 11.2–16. The first step in such a reassess-
ment occurred at the 2000 Annual Meeting of the Society of Biblical
Literature in Nashville, Tennessee, in a session of the Christian Apocrypha
Section that was entirely dedicated to a discussion of "Mary(s) in Christian
Apocrypha." In a paper prepared for this session entitled "The Portrait of
Mary in the *Ascension of Isaiah,*"[13] Jonathan Knight presented the case for
a reevaluation of the portrait of Mary in the early church based upon all
the available sources, both canonical and noncanonical.[14] Knight rightly
called attention to the sensitive ecclesiastical and dogmatic issues that may
have impeded such a venture in the past[15] and concluded that "the time is
ripe for the reconsideration of Mary's place in the contours of early Christian history and theology."[16]

   Unfortunately, the Marian witness of *Ascen. Isa.* 11.2–16 is part of a
section of the document that is plagued by textual problems. *Ascension of
Isaiah* 11.2–22 occurs only in the Ethiopic text of the pseudepigraphon and
is absent from the Slavonic and part of the Latin manuscript tradition.[17] The
primary argument in favor of the authenticity of *Ascen. Isa.* 11.2–22 is that
the Ethiopic text generally seems to be more reliable than the Slavic and
Latin manuscripts that omit these verses. Furthermore, an important Greek
papyrus fragment of the fifth or sixth century C.E.,[18] wherever it is extant,

---

[13] Pp. 91–105 in the present volume.

[14] Knight's contribution is the latest expression of the contemporary "reasonable
consensus" in support of an early date and unified composition for the *Ascension
of Isaiah* with "the obvious corollary that the *Ascension of Isaiah* ranks among our
earliest noncanonical Christian literature" (Knight, "Mary," 93).

[15] "No longer is it true to say that Protestants turn their backs on Mary
because of the position she enjoys in Roman Catholic theology. Nor do Roman
Catholics neglect the Bible when it comes to their evaluation of the mother of
God" (ibid., 91).

[16] Ibid.

[17] See the detailed discussion by Joseph Verheyden, "L'Ascension d'Isaïe et
L'Évangile de Matthieu: Examen de AI 3,13–18," in *The New Testament in Early
Christianity: La réception des écrits néotestamentaires dans le christianisme
primitif* (ed. J.-M. Sevrin; BETL 86; Leuven: Leuven University Press, 1989),
247–74.

[18] Bernard P. Grenfell and Arthur S. Hunt, *The Ascension of Isaiah and Other
Theological Fragments, with Nine Plates* (part 1 of *The Amherst Papyri, Being an
Account of the Greek Papyri in the Collection of the Right Hon. Lord Amherst of
Hackney, F.S.A. at Didlington Hall, Norfolk* (London: Oxford University Press,
1900), 1–22; Enrico Norelli, "Frammento greco dell'Ascensione di Isaia (Papiro
Amherst 1): Introduzione, edizione e traduzione," in Bettiolo et al., *Ascensio Isa-
iae: Textus,* 133–45.

generally supports the Ethiopic text, thus suggesting that the papyrus might also verify the Ethiopic witness of *Ascen. Isa.* 11.2–16.[19]

Most scholars accept the authenticity of the Marian material in *Ascen. Isa.* 11.2–16 in spite of the textual issues involved.[20] Jonathan Knight has been a persistent proponent of the originality of *Ascen. Isa.* 11.2–22, and of its Marian witness in verses 2–16, for two basic reasons. First, according to Knight, this material shares a common outlook and certain distinctive ideas with similar material found in the first section of the apocalypse (3.13–18). Second, Knight finds it reasonable to assume that a later "orthodox" editor could have expunged the Marian passage because of its seemingly docetic character, thus leading to the abbreviated text of *Ascen. Isa.* 11 found in the Slavic and Latin manuscript tradition.[21] Knight concludes: "It is very substantially easier to see *Ascen. Isa.* 11.2–22, with all its warts, as part of the original apocalypse than to treat it as later hagiography."[22]

The probable existence of an authentic passage containing advanced Mariological material that is dated to the early second century C.E. necessarily raises critical questions pertaining to the possible sources of this material and to its place within the milieu of early Christian literature. Knight's discussion regarding the position of the Marian section of the *Ascension of Isaiah* in early Christianity centers, first, around its relationship to the canonical Gospel of Matthew, which is the earliest known written witness to an elevated Mariology. Some scholars maintain that the *Ascension of Isaiah* was influenced by Matthew, while others ascribe the relationship to a mutual dependence upon earlier traditions.[23] Knight also discusses in detail the work of Bauckham on the phenomenon of "kerygmatic summaries" in early Christian literature.[24] Bauckham assigns the Christian material in *Ascen. Isa.* 3.13–18; 9.13–18; 10.17–11:33 (including the crucial Marian witness in *Ascen. Isa.* 11.2–16) to what he calls the "kerygmatic summary" tradition.[25]

---

[19] Pier Cesare Bori, "L'estasi del profeta: *Ascensio Isaiae* 6 e l'antico profetismo cristiano," *CNS* 1 (1980): 367–89, comes to this conclusion regarding *Ascen. Isa.* 6.

[20] Bauckham, "Summaries," 192–97; idem, "Ascension," 379; Knight, *Ascension,* 75; idem, *Disciples,* 26–27; Norelli, *Ascensio Isaiae: Commentarius,* 42–43, 535–38; Hannah, "Vision," 86; Hall, "Ascent," 483 (with reservations).

[21] Knight, "Mary," 97; idem, *Disciples,* 66.

[22] Knight, "Mary," 97.

[23] See Knight's summary and references in "Mary," 98–99.

[24] Bauckham, "Summaries," 185–217; Knight, "Mary," 97–98; idem, *Disciples,* 274–78, 288–89.

[25] Bauckham, "Summaries," 191–204.

Bauckham describes "kerygmatic summaries" as a new, more flexible genre of Christian traditions characterized by their mythological quality in presenting Jesus as a divine being who has died in this world only to arise and ascend to an exalted position in heaven; he distinguishes this genre from the plain, fixed, narrative descriptions of Jesus found in the written and oral Gospel tradition. By identifying verbal points of contact in the "kerygmatic summaries" occurring in various canonical and noncanonical documents, and in other early Christian writers,[26] Bauckham has located "a common stock" of such material in Christian antiquity from which individual literary units were composed. According to Bauckham, the author of the *Ascension of Isaiah* "did not compose his summaries of the history of Jesus directly from the written Gospels or from the oral Gospel traditions, but followed a traditional pattern of kerygmatic summary which narrated the history of Jesus in a series of brief statements."[27]

Bauckham presents much compelling evidence in support of his "kerygmatic summary" theory that may explain, or at least illuminate, certain aspects of the early Jesus traditions, including those found in the three such summaries that he has identified in *Ascen. Isa.* 3.13–4.18; 9.13–18; and 10.17–11.33. However, it would be a mistake to assign the Marian passage *Ascen. Isa.* 11.2–16 to the "kerygmatic summary" category,[28] at least in its earliest pre-Gospel phase. Although it may be true that the three passages in question share the same mythological-christological framework with each other and contain material and language that is typical of other "kerygmatic summaries,"[29] Bauckham himself admits that in *Ascen. Isa.* 11.2–15 the author of the *Ascension of Isaiah* "has broken out of the form of kerygmatic summary altogether, and told this part of the history of Jesus in full narrative form."[30] Thus, the passage in the *Ascension of Isaiah* that contains the crucial Marian material under discussion is excluded from Bauckham's "kerygmatic summaries" category and, therefore, could not be part of the oral traditions circulating in the pre-Gospel stage.

Bauckham provides an explanation for this seeming inconsistency in his theory when he attempts to demonstrate the antiquity of his "kerygmatic summary" tradition by establishing a connection to what he calls "the one unquestionably very early kerygmatic summary we have (1 Cor. 15:3–7)."[31] However, Bauckham seems to have used later sources, such as the

---

[26] Ibid., 191–213, contains numerous specific references.
[27] Ibid., 201.
[28] Ibid., 193.
[29] Ibid., 195, 199.
[30] Ibid., 203.
[31] Ibid., 211.

Kerygma Petrou, Justin, and Irenaeus, to delineate the parameters of his "kerygmatic summary" tradition of Jesus (coming-birth-suffering/death-resurrection-assumption to heaven).[32] But 1 Cor 15:3–7 refers only to the death, burial, resurrection, and postresurrection appearances of Jesus and does not mention Mary or anything having to do with the nativity. Bauckham attempts to justify this omission with the rationalization that "Paul cites that part of the summary which is relevant to his purpose: a discussion of resurrection. There is no reason why Paul should not have known a form in which it was usual to summarize the ministry of Jesus as well as his death and resurrection."[33] Such an argument from silence must be rejected. The fact remains that there is no known source for the events surrounding the birth of Jesus in the pre-Gospel tradition.

The same dilemma confronts Bauckham when he attempts to trace the persistence of his "kerygmatic summary" tradition by "establishing that the kerygmatic summaries in the speeches of Acts belong to the same, broad, and diverse tradition of kerygmatic summaries of which a variety of other early Christian writings preserve evidence."[34] The fifth point of Bauckham's conclusions is particularly germane to our present discussion. He notes that "the kerygmatic summaries in Acts begin no earlier than the ministry of John the Baptist (10.37; 13.24). They do not refer to the birth of Jesus, still less his coming into the world."[35] Bauckham then again refers to a series of later documents to demonstrate that "nearly all other kerygmatic summaries we have noticed refer to Christ's birth."[36] The first, and therefore oldest, of these proof texts for the authenticity of the birth of Christ as an element in the "kerygmatic summary" tradition is *Ascen. Isa.* 11.2–16! Bauckham again resorts to the argument from silence to support the nonexistence of the birth element in the "kerygmatic summaries" in Acts: "It seems likely that kerygmatic summaries beginning with the birth of Jesus go back to Luke's time. If so, he has chosen not to follow these in the speeches of Acts."[37] The fact still remains. There is no known source for the events surrounding the birth of Jesus in the pre-Gospel tradition.

---

[32] Ibid.

[33] Ibid.

[34] Ibid., 213.

[35] Ibid., 215.

[36] Ibid.

[37] Ibid., 216. Bauckham's statement that Luke's Gospel "takes the story of Jesus back to his conception" cannot be used to support the presence of the birth element in the "kerygmatic summaries" of Luke's time because of the questions surrounding the origin and character of Luke's infancy stories.

In his own evaluation of the relationship between Bauckham's "keryg-matic summaries" in the *Ascension of Isaiah* and the "crystallizing Gospel tradition of the New Testament," Knight accepts the validity of the form of the "kerygmatic summary" as a genre, but stops short of acknowledging direct Matthean influence on the content of the *Ascension of Isaiah*'s "kerygmatic summaries."[38] While not ruling out the possibility that the author of the *Ascension of Isaiah* may have known Matthew's Gospel, Knight takes a strong position that "there is most certainly a connection between the *Ascension of Isaiah* and Matthew's *special material. . . .* This connection does not necessarily mean that the author used Matthew itself. He could have drawn on the source that provided Matthew's special mate-rial so that it is not proven to posit direct literary dependence in explanation of the facts in question. The latter argument is accepted as convincing by Norelli in particular."[39]

Therefore, the current state of the question of the origin of the Marian material in *Ascen. Isa.* 11 seems to be that this passage may have originated in an oral tradition, or a written source, that possibly predated, and perhaps was even used by, the canonical gospels themselves. Knight concludes:

> the evidence of *Ascen. Isa.* 11.2–22 in the Ethiopic version suggests that the author used a pre-Matthean source for the summaries that Matthew also utilized. This is an important conclusion for studying the Marian tra-ditions in the apocalypse. It shows that, even if chapters 6–11 come from the second century C.E., they incorporate earlier material so that we are placed in touch with traditions about Jesus that circulated in the first cen-tury C.E., evidently before the writing of the canonical gospels.[40]

Knight has long advocated the possible existence of earlier, non-Gospel sources of at least some of the Marian material in *Ascen. Isa.* 11.2–16. He identified an "evident seam" between *Ascen. Isa.* 11.22 and 23 that "is a good indication that the author was drawing on a source in 11.2–22 (as he did in 3.13–18)."[41]

---

[38] Knight, "Mary," 97–98. See also his discussion in *Disciples,* 276–78, 288, where he seemed closer to accepting such influence.

[39] Knight, "Mary," 99. In an earlier study, *Ascension,* 15, he stated that "the min-istry of Jesus is described in language which shows knowledge of Matthew's special material (3.13–18) and of broader traditions as well (cf. also '11:2–22 in the Ethiopic text')."

[40] Knight, "Mary," 100.

[41] Knight, *Disciples,* 68. See also his *Ascension,* 84: "The traditions about Jesus are inserted into the context of the mediator's descent in 3.13–18 and 11.2–22 and were originally separate from it."

This source, however, is never identified, much less associated with the *Protevangelium of James*. It seems to be a given among scholars that the *Protevangelium of James* is irrelevant to any discussion about traditions of the late first and early second centuries c.e. The *Protevangelium of James* is mentioned only occasionally in the scholarly debate on the Marian segment in *Ascen. Isa.* 11.2–16 and usually as a secondary witness to what are assumed to be later developments in Marian teaching.[42] A typical statement of the universally accepted position on the relation between the *Ascension of Isaiah* and the *Protevangelium of James* is: "The *Ascension of Isaiah* provides early evidence for the belief that Mary remained a virgin following the birth of Jesus (11.9). This idea was repeated in the later *Protevangelium of James* (c. 150 CE), which said that Mary's birth, like Jesus', was divinely ordained."[43] The *Protevangelium of James* is not even mentioned in Knight's 355-page comprehensive treatment of the *Ascension of Isaiah*.[44]

In the following discussion of Knight's assessment of the Marian traditions in the *Ascension of Isaiah,* which he describes as "the real content of this paper,"[45] I will attempt to supplement and complement his position with information from the perspective of my research on the *Protevangelium of James*. In my opinion, many of the questions left unanswered in the treatment of the Marian passage in *Ascen. Isa.* 11 by Knight and others may at least be illuminated, if not actually resolved, by the new perspective on the *Protevangelium of James* that I presented to the Christian Apocrypha Section in 1994 and 1997.[46] Valuable insights concerning the subject at hand may be gained from consideration of the possibility that one of the source documents of the *Protevangelium of James*, which I called the *Genesis Marias*[47] in my 1997 paper,[48] was already in existence as early as the late first or early second centuries c.e. As a result of this research, the position of Knight and the other scholars who advocate an early date for the *Ascension of Isaiah* would gain strong support from the existence of another early witness to the same Marian themes that distinguish the *Ascension of Isaiah*.

---

[42] See, for example, Hall, "Ascent," 483.

[43] Knight, *Ascension,* 88.

[44] Knight, *Disciples.*

[45] Knight, "Mary," 100.

[46] Published in the *SBL Seminar Papers* in 1994 (Zervos, "Dating") and 1997 (idem, "Annunciation").

[47] This is part of the actual title of the *Protevangelium of James* in the third- or fourth-century P.Bod. V, which contains a complete text of this document.

[48] Zervos, "Annunciation," 666, 686–88.

It was mentioned above that there were certain elements in the Marian material in *Ascen. Isa.* 11 that did not originate in the canonical Gospel tradition. These were Mary's Davidic descent, her astonishment at the miraculous appearance of the infant Jesus, her short two-month pregnancy, the absence of a midwife in the nativity, and Mary's *virginitas post partum*. It was partly on the basis of the existence of two such noncanonical elements in the *Ascension of Isaiah* that Knight rejected the exclusive dependence of the *Ascension of Isaiah* on Matthew alone. The first was the "strange description of the resurrection in *Ascen. Isa.* 3:16–17 (see *Gos. Pet.* 34–42)"; the second concerned "the absent midwife in *Ascen. Isa.* 11:14."[49] Knight rightly substantiates his first example with a reference to the *Gospel of Peter* but is silent on any non-Matthean parallels to his second example. Actually, the absent midwife in *Ascen. Isa.* 11.14 is an important contact with *Prot. Jas.* 19, which narrates the birth of Jesus. In *Prot. Jas.* 17–18 Mary is about to give birth on the road to Bethlehem. Joseph puts her in a cave and goes out in search of a Hebrew midwife to assist in the birth. By the time they arrive at the cave in *Prot. Jas.* 19.12–15, the child has already appeared. This is the first of the striking parallels between the *Ascension of Isaiah* Marian materials and the *Protevangelium of James*.

A second extra-Matthean Marian element contained in the *Ascension of Isaiah* is that Mary is a descendant of the house of David. Knight attributes this element to the second century and describes it as an attempt to improve upon what is known about Joseph's Davidic ancestry from Matthew in order to enhance Jesus' messianic qualifications.[50] I agree that this appears to represent an attempt to improve over Matthew's genealogy but question why it has to be placed as late as the second century. However, the relationship between Matthew and *Ascension of Isaiah* must be revisited first. If, as Knight seems to have concluded above, the author of *Ascension of Isaiah* did not know Matthew, then how could he know and respond to Matthew's genealogy? And even if, against Bauckham himself, *Ascen. Isa.* 11.2–22 is a "kerygmatic summary" from preexisting non-Matthean material, it seems a stronger case can be made for an even earlier date for this Marian element. It must have been established in Syria before about 110 C.E., since Ignatius already knows of Mary's Davidic descent quite early in the second century.[51]

Since this second non-Matthean element in the *Ascension of Isaiah* also occurs in *Prot. Jas.* 10.2, there are solid grounds for regarding the Davidic

---

[49] Knight, "Mary," 99.

[50] Ibid., 100–101.

[51] Ign., *Eph.* 18.2; 20.2; *Trall.* 9.1; *Smyrn.* 1.1.

descent of Mary to have been part of an early tradition or source that informed the *Ascension of Isaiah,* Ignatius, and the *Protevangelium of James.* Assuming that Ignatius himself did not create the idea of Mary's Davidic descent, it would be difficult to demonstrate definitively whether the *Ascension of Isaiah* or the *Protevangelium of James* contains a more original version of this element. Whereas *Ascen. Isa.* 11.2 very tersely states only that Isaiah saw a "woman of the progeny of David the prophet," *Prot. Jas.* 10.2 weaves this piece of information into a story of the making of the temple veil. And if Bauckham is correct, and *Ascen. Isa.* 11.2–22 is not from an oral "kerygmatic summary" but from a written source in "full narrative form,"[52] then what other such source would have existed that early, that is, before Ignatius and the *Ascension of Isaiah,* and with the specific content of Mary's Davidic ancestry, other than the *Genesis Marias,* the document that was later incorporated into the *Protevangelium of James?*

The next element to be examined in the *Ascension of Isaiah* Marian text is "that Joseph was dissuaded from divorcing Mary through an angelophany and that he had no sexual relations with her before the birth of Jesus."[53] Knight quickly dispenses with this passage as being Matthean in thought, although he accepts the language used as being peculiar to the *Ascension of Isaiah.* The basic theme of the passage does seem to be Matthean, but some parts of the text warrant closer inspection, especially with respect to the parallel text in chapters 13–14 of the *Protevangelium of James.* But any comparison of the two texts is problematic because the corresponding section in the *Protevangelium of James* has been heavily edited by the addition of Matthean elements to such an extent that one can discern only with difficulty the underlying *Genesis Marias* material.[54] The purpose of the later *Protevangelium of James* editor was precisely to bring his source document, the *Genesis Marias,* into conformity with the Matthean Joseph story.

However, the *Ascension of Isaiah* story contains some interesting affinities with the vestiges of the *Genesis Marias* tradition that are still discernible in the *Protevangelium of James.* First, *Ascen. Isa.* 11.2 refers to Joseph as a carpenter, which is not a particularly Matthean concept. Matthew 13:55 also describes Joseph as a carpenter, but this is not original to Matthew and is not associated with Matthew's birth story. This information has been taken and modified from Matthew's source, Mark 6:3, where Jesus is portrayed as a carpenter. The parallels in *Prot. Jas.* 9 and 13 again are built into the *Protevangelium of James* narrative, which presents Joseph

---

[52] Bauckham, "Summaries," 203.

[53] Knight, "Mary," 101.

[54] Zervos, "Annunciation," 422–25.

very strongly as being employed in construction. Even more significantly, *Ascen. Isa.* 11.9 shares with the *Protevangelium of James* the important non-Matthean element of the *virginitas post partum*.[55] Quite interesting also is *Ascen. Isa.* 11.3, which states that "Joseph came into his portion."[56] The reference to Joseph's portion, or lot, occurs in *Prot. Jas.* 9, where Joseph is chosen by lot to be Mary's guardian. Joseph's "lot" as well as the reference to Joseph as a carpenter are in a demonstrably *Genesis Marias* section of *Prot. Jas.* 9. Again the cumulative evidence of these parallels between the *Protevangelium of James* and the *Ascension of Isaiah* in this Marian element point to the narrative of the *Genesis Marias* as a possible source of at least some of the Marian information in the *Ascension of Isaiah*.

Another Marian element in this "kerygmatic summary" in *Ascen. Isa.* 11 is the description of the birth of Jesus, which according to Knight "is strikingly different from Matthew's account."[57] In *Ascen. Isa.* 11.8 Mary gave birth to Jesus after being pregnant only two months. Moreover, the birth itself apparently took the mother by surprise. Here, Knight does note the parallel in *Prot. Jas.* 13.1, which states that Mary gave birth in the sixth month of her pregnancy. However, one of the main themes in my 1997 paper, which was actually entitled "An Early Non-canonical Annunciation Story," is that in the annunciation story of the *Genesis Marias* Mary was not informed of her impending pregnancy by the voice of the annunciation. She only became aware of this later and was perplexed when her womb began to swell. Knight attributes this supernatural birth of Jesus in the *Ascension of Isaiah* to the author's desire to emphasize the supernatural character of Jesus. This may be true with respect to the present position of this story in the *Ascension of Isaiah,* but may not hold true for the original source of this story, which may have been the *Genesis Marias*.

Probably the most important single Mariological element in the Marian section of the *Ascension of Isaiah* is the *virginitas post partum* of Mary, which is nowhere to be found in the canonical birth narratives of Matthew and Luke. Knight comes close to attributing the responsibility for the creation of this idea to the author of the *Ascension of Isaiah,*[58] even though Knight himself notes the significant parallel in *Prot. Jas.* 19–20,[59] where it is graphically stated that the midwife physically examined Mary after the birth of Jesus and determined that she was still a virgin. Knight further notes that *Ascen. Isa.* 11.14 states that no midwife attended Jesus' birth but

---

[55] See discussion below.

[56] Knibb, "Martyrdom," 174, translates this as "lot."

[57] Knight, "Mary," 101.

[58] Ibid., 102.

[59] Ibid.

again attributes this to the author's desire to enhance Jesus. This also may hold true for the present position of this element in the *Ascension of Isaiah,* but it is also true that in the birth narrative of the *Protevangelium of James,* where Mary is the central figure, the midwife did not arrive in time to attend the birth of Jesus. This is yet another impressive example where the author of the *Ascension of Isaiah* may have taken an element from the source of the *Protevangelium of James* and inserted it into his own birth narrative, where there is more of an emphasis on Jesus as the mythological descending-ascending redeemer from the seventh heaven.

In evaluating the Marian material in the *Ascension of Isaiah* with a view to its contacts with other Christian literature describing the birth of Jesus, Knight sees two principal developments over the Gospel tradition: first, the spontaneous birth of Jesus that escapes Mary's notice and causes her astonishment when she sees the infant who has suddenly appeared, and, secondly, the fact that Mary was found to be a virgin after her delivery.[60] Both of these elements are part of the principal focus of the *Protevangelium of James* and of its source, the *Genesis Marias.* Knight interprets both of these as christological statements reflecting the belief that Jesus is the earthly manifestation of the divine mediator who descended from heaven. Knight asks the critical question *cui bono,* "to whose advantage these additions are made: to Jesus' or to Mary's."[61] He rejects the latter possibility and maintains that these additions point beyond the person of Mary to the Beloved One. Knight then rightly concludes by contrasting the *Protevangelium of James,* which is decidedly written for the advantage of Mary, with the *Ascension of Isaiah,* whose entire framework is the myth of the descending-ascending redeemer.

It is precisely with regard to Knight's final questions and conclusions that the *Protevangelium of James* can be most instructive. Why should the author of the *Ascension of Isaiah* want to write about Mary in this way, especially if this author was most concerned with the heavenly redeemer Jesus? I would add a further question. Does Mary's *post partum* virginity and her astonishment at giving birth to Jesus enhance Jesus, or does it enhance Mary? The answer to these questions perhaps betrays the real source of the Marian material in the *Ascension of Isaiah.* I would agree with Knight that the author of the *Ascension of Isaiah* inserted material in his "kerygmatic summary" according to his christological scheme. But I would look elsewhere for the source of the seemingly unnecessary Marian material in the *Ascension of Isaiah.* I would look to a document, or a tradition, independent of the not-yet-canonical gospels, that had as its purpose

---

[60] Ibid., 103.
[61] Ibid.

precisely the enhancement of the person of Mary. I would look to a document that contained all the elements in the *Ascension of Isaiah* representing a departure from, or a development of, the Matthean Marian elements in this apocalypse. I would look to the *Protevangelium of James* and its underlying source document, the *Genesis Marias*.

Knight can only arrive at his conclusions concerning the Marian material in *Ascen. Isa.* 11 after taking as a "given that the *Ascension of Isaiah* is earlier than the *Protevangelium of James*,"[62] which he dismisses as later "apocryphal Marian hagiography."[63] This "given" reflects the perception of most contemporary scholars that is based upon an outdated, but still well-entrenched, scholarly consensus that views the *Protevangelium of James* as a monolithic composition written in the middle to latter part of the second century C.E. whose value for earlier Christology and Mariology is not worth serious consideration. We should remember that the *Ascension of Isaiah* was branded with a similar set of misperceptions only a few short years ago. The *Protevangelium of James* has not had the benefit of international teams of scholars working arduously for decades to produce thorough critical editions of its text with accompanying exhaustive commentaries and volumes of extensive critical evaluations. Should such study of the *Protevangelium of James* come about in the future, this document will doubtless be identified as an invaluable and unique witness to the thought of earliest Christianity and will be recognized, even in its present heavily redacted form, as being at least equal in importance to the *Ascension of Isaiah*. And the *Genesis Marias,* in my opinion, will prove to be the primary source document of the Mariology of the ancient Christian world whose ideas were reflected in such later writings as the *Protevangelium of James, Ascen. Isa.* 11.2–16, and the letters of Ignatius of Antioch.

---

[62] Ibid., 104.

[63] Ibid., 105.

Select Bibliography

Ann Graham Brock

Albertz, Martin. "Über die Christophanie der Mutter Jesu." *TSK* 86 (1913): 483–516.

Albrecht, Ruth. "Maria." *DNP* 7:887–90.

Allberry, C. R. C. *A Manichaean Psalm-Book: Part II*. Manichaean Manuscripts in the Chester Beatty Collection 2. Stuttgart: Kohlhammer, 1938.

Amsler, Frédéric. *Acta Philippi: Commentarius*. CCSA 12. Turnhout: Brepols, 1999.

Atwood, Richard. *Mary Magdalene in the New Testament Gospels and Early Tradition*. European University Studies 457. Bern: Lang, 1993.

Baarda, Tjitze. *Aphrahat's Text of the Fourth Gospel*. Vol. 1 of *The Gospel Quotations of Aphrahat the Persian Sage*. Amsterdam: Vrije Universiteit Amsterdam, 1975.

———. "Jesus and Mary (John 20:16f.) in the Second Epistle on Virginity Ascribed to Clement." Pages 87–110 in *Essays on the Diatessaron*. Kampen: Pharos, 1994.

Bieberstein, Sabine. *Verschwiegene Jüngerinnen—vergessene Zeuginnen: Gebrochene Konzepte im Lukasevangelium*. NTOA 38. Fribourg: Universitätsverlag; Göttingen: Vandenhoeck & Ruprecht, 1998.

Boer, Esther de. *Mary Magdalene: Beyond the Myth*. Translated by John Bowden. Harrisburg, Pa.: Trinity Press International, 1997.

Bouvier, Bertrand, and François Bovon. "Actes de Philippe, I, d'après un manuscrit inédit." Pages 367–94 in *Oecumenica et Patristica: Festschrift für Wilhelm Schneemelcher*. Edited by Damaskinos Papandreou, Wolfgang A. Bienert, and Knut Schäferdiek. Geneva: Metropolie der Schweiz, 1989.

Bovon, François. "Les Actes de Philippe." *ANRW* 2.25.6:4432–4525.

———. "Le privilège pascal de Marie-Madeleine." *NTS* 30 (1984): 50–62, translated as "Mary Magdalene's Paschal Privilege." Pages 147–57, 228–35 in *New Testament Traditions and Apocryphal Narratives*. Translated by Jane Haapiseva-Hunter. PTMS 36. Allison Park, Pa.: Pickwick, 1995.

Bovon, François, Bertrand Bouvier, and Frédéric Amsler. *Acta Philippi: Textus*. CCSA 11. Turnhout: Brepols, 1999.

Brock, Ann Graham. "Authority, Politics, and Gender in Early Christianity: Mary, Peter, and the Portrayal of Leadership." Ph.D. diss., Harvard University, 2000.

———. *Mary Magdalene, the First Apostle: The Struggle for Authority.* HTS 51. Cambridge: Harvard University Press, 2002.

———. "Peter, Paul, and Mary: Canonical vs. Non-canonical Portrayals of Apostolic Witnesses." Pages 173–202 in *SBL Seminar Papers, 1999.* SBLSP 38. Atlanta: Society of Biblical Literature, 1999.

Brooten, Bernadette. "'Junia ... Outstanding among the Apostles' (Romans 16:7)." Pages 141–44 in *Women Priests: A Catholic Commentary on the Vatican Declaration.* Edited by Leonard Swidler and Arlene Swidler. New York: Paulist, 1977.

Brown, Raymond E. "Roles of Women in the Fourth Gospel." *TS* 36 (1975): 688–99.

Brown, Raymond E., et al., eds. *Mary in the New Testament: A Collaborative Assessment by Protestant and Roman Catholic Scholars.* New York: Paulist, 1978.

Brown, Raymond E., Karl Donfried, and J. Reumann, eds. *Peter in the New Testament: A Collaborative Assessment by Protestant and Roman Catholic Scholars.* Minneapolis: Augsburg; New York: Paulist, 1973.

Buck, F. "Are the 'Ascension of Isaiah' and the 'Odes of Solomon' Witnesses to an Early Cult of Mary?" Pages 371–99 in vol. 4 of *De primordiis cultu mariani.* Rome: Pontificia academia mariana internationalis, 1970.

Buckley, Jorunn Jacobson. *Female Fault and Fulfilment in Gnosticism.* Studies in Religion. Chapel Hill: University of North Carolina Press, 1986.

———. "An Interpretation of Logion 114 in *The Gospel of Thomas.*" *NovT* 27 (1985): 245–72.

———. "The Mandaean Appropriation of Jesus' Mother, Miriai." *NovT* 35 (1993): 181–96.

Campenhausen, Hans von. *The Virgin Birth in the Theology of the Ancient Church.* Translated by Frank Clarke. SHT 2. London: SCM, 1964.

Collins, Raymond. "Mary." *ABD* 4:584–86.

Cooper, Kate. "Apostles, Ascetic Women, and Questions of Audience: New Reflections on the Rhetoric of Gender in the Apocryphal Acts." Pages 147–53 in *SBL Seminar Papers, 1992.* SBLSP 31. Atlanta: Scholars Press, 1992.

Coyle, J. Kevin. "Mary Magdalene in Manichaeism?" *Mus* 104 (1991): 39–55.

D'Angelo, Mary Rose. "Re-membering Jesus: Women, Prophecy, and Resistance in the Memory of the Early Churches." *Hor* 19.2 (1990): 199–218.

Derrett, J. Duncan M. "Miriam and the Resurrection (John 20,16)." *DRev* 111 (1993): 174–86.

Devos, P. "L'apparition du Resuscité à sa Mère: Un nouveau témoin copte." *AnBoll* 96 (1978): 388.

Eisen, Ute E. *Women Officeholders in Early Christianity: Epigraphical and Literary Studies.* Translated by Linda M. Maloney. Collegeville, Minn.: Liturgical Press, 2000.

Elliott, James Keith. *The Apocryphal New Testament: A Collection of Apocryphal Christian Literature in an English Translation.* Oxford: Clarendon, 1993.

Emmel, Stephen, ed. *Nag Hammadi Codex III,5: The Dialogue of the Savior.* Introduction by Helmut Koester and Elaine Pagels. NHS 26. Leiden: Brill, 1984.

Erbetta, Mario. *Atti e leggende.* Vol. 2.2 of *Gli apocrifi del Nuovo Testamento.* Turin: Marietti, 1966.

———. *Vangeli.* Vol. 1.2 of *Gli apocrifi del Nuovo Testamento.* Turin: Marietti, 1981.

Esbroeck, Michel van. "Apocryphes géorgiens de la Dormition." *AnBoll* 92 (1973): 55–75.

———. "Les textes littéraires sur l'assomption avant le Xe siècle." Pages 265–85 in François Bovon et al., *Les actes apocryphes des apôtres.* Geneva: Labor et Fides, 1981.

Gaventa, Beverly Roberts. *Mary: Glimpses of the Mother of Jesus.* Columbia: University of South Carolina Press, 1995; Minneapolis: Fortress, 1999.

Giannelli, C. "Témoignages patristiques grecs en faveur d'une apparition du Christ ressuscité à la Vierge Marie." In *Mélanges M. Jugie, REByz* 11 (1953): 106–19.

Good, Deirdre. "Pistis Sophia." Pages 678–707 in vol. 2 of *Searching the Scriptures: A Feminist Commentary.* Edited by Elisabeth Schüssler Fiorenza. 2 vols. New York: Crossroad, 1993–94.

Graef, Hilda. *Mary: A History of Doctrine and Devotion.* 2 vols. New York: Sheed & Ward, 1963.

Harnack, Adolf von. *Untersuchungen über das gnostische Buch Pistis Sophia.* TU 7.2. Leipzig: Hinrichs, 1891.

Hartenstein, Judith. *Die zweite Lehre: Erscheinungen des Auferstandenen als Rahmenerzählungen frühchristlicher Dialoge.* TU 146. Berlin: Akademie, 2000.

Haskins, Susan. *Mary Magdalene: Myth and Metaphor.* New York: Harcourt Brace & Co., 1993.

Hedrick, Charles, and Robert Hodgson Jr., eds. *Nag Hammadi, Gnosticism, and Early Christianity.* Peabody, Mass.: Hendrickson, 1986.

Heine, Susanne. *Women and Early Christianity: Are the Feminist Scholars Right?* Translated by John Bowden. London: SCM, 1987.

Hengel, Martin. "Maria Magdalena und die Frauen als Zeugen." Pages 243–56 in *Abraham unser Vater: Juden und Christen im Gespräch über die Bibel: Festschrift für Otto Michel zum 60. Geburtstag.* Edited by Otto Betz, Martin Hengel, and Peter Schmidt. Leiden: Brill, 1963.

Holl, Karl. "Der Kirchenbegriff des Paulus in seinem Verhältnis zu dem der Urgemeinde (1921)." Pages 44–67 in vol. 2 of *Gesammelte Aufsätze zur Kirchengeschichte.* Tübingen: Mohr Siebeck, 1928. Repr., Darmstadt: Wissenschaftliche Buchgesellschaft, 1964.

Holzmeister, Urban. "Die Magdalenenfrage in der kirchlichen Überlieferung." *ZKT* 46 (1922): 402–22, 556–84.

Isenberg, Wesley W., intro. and trans. "The Gospel of Philip (II,3)." Pages 139–60 in *NHL*.

James, Montague Rhodes. *The Apocryphal New Testament.* Oxford: Clarendon, 1924.

King, Karen. "Canonization and Marginalization: Mary of Magdala." Pages 29–36 in *Women's Sacred Scriptures.* Edited by Kwok Pui-Lan and Elisabeth Schüssler Fiorenza. Concilium. Revue internationale de théologie 1998.3. London: SCM; Maryknoll: Orbis, 1998.

———. "The Gospel of Mary." Pages 357–66 in *The Complete Gospels: Annotated Scholars Version.* Edited by Robert J. Miller. Rev. and exp. ed. Sonoma, Calif.: Polebridge, 1994.

———. "The Gospel of Mary Magdalene." Pages 601–34 in vol. 2 of *Searching the Scriptures.* Edited by Elisabeth Schüssler Fiorenza. 2 vols. New York: Crossroad, 1993–94.

———. *The Gospel of Mary.* Santa Rosa, Calif.: Polebridge, forthcoming.

———. "Introduction" [to the *Gospel of Mary* (BG 8502, 1)]. Pages 523–24 in *NHL*.

———. "Prophetic Power and Women's Authority: The Case of the Gospel of Mary Magdalene." Pages 21–41, 357–66 in *Women Preachers and Prophets through Two Millenia of Christianity.* Edited by Beverly Mayne Kienzle and Pamela J. Walker. Berkeley and Los Angeles: University of California Press, 1998.

Kitzberger, Ingrid Rosa. "Mary of Bethany and Mary of Magdala—Two Female Characters in the Johannine Passion Narrative: A Feminist, Narrative-Critical Reader-Response." *NTS* 41 (1995): 564–86.

Knight, Jonathan. *The Ascension of Isaiah.* Guides to Apocrypha and Pseudepigrapha 2. Sheffield: Sheffield Academic Press, 1995.

Koester, Helmut. *Ancient Christian Gospels: Their History and Development.* Philadelphia: Trinity Press International, 1992.

———. "Introduction [to *The Gospel according to Thomas*]." Pages 38–49 in *Nag Hammadi Codex II,2–7.* Edited by Bentley Layton. NHS 20. Leiden: Brill, 1989.

———. "La tradition apostolique et les origines du gnosticisme." *RTP* 119 (1987): 1–16.

Koester, Helmut, and Elaine Pagels. "Introduction [to *The Dialogue of the Savior*]." In *Nag Hammadi Codex III,5: The Dialogue of the Savior.* Edited by Stephen Emmel. NHS 26. Leiden: Brill, 1984.

Lacau, Pierre. *Fragments d'apocryphes coptes.* Vol. 9 of *Mémoires publiés par les membres de l'institut français d'archéologie orientale du Caire.* Cairo: Imprimerie de l'institut français d'archéologie orientale, 1904.

Layton, Bentley. *The Gnostic Scriptures.* Garden City, N.Y.: Doubleday, 1987.

Leloir, Louis. *Éphrem de Nisibe: Commentaire de l'évangile concordant ou Diatessaron traduit du syriaque et de l'arménien.* SC 121. Paris: Cerf, 1966.

Lemm, Oscar von. "Koptische apokryphe Apostelacten." *Mélanges asiatiques* 10 (1890–92): 110–47.

Lipsius, Richard Adelbert. *Die apokryphen Apostelgeschichten und Apostellegenden.* 2 vols. in 3 and supp. 1883–90. Repr., Amsterdam: Philo, 1976.

Lipsius, Richard Adelbert, and Maximilianus Bonnet. *Acta apostolorum apocrypha.* 2 vols in 3. Leipzig: Mendelssohn, 1891–1903. Repr., Darmstadt: Wissenschaftliche Buchgesellschaft, 1959.

Lucchesi, Enzo. "Évangile selon Marie ou Évangile selon Marie-Madeleine?" *AnBoll* 103 (1985): 366.

Lührmann, Dieter. "Die griechischen Fragmente des Mariaevangeliums POxy 3525 und PRyl 463." *NovT* 30 (1988): 321–38.

MacDonald, Margaret Y. *Early Christian Women and Pagan Opinion: The Power of the Hysterical Woman.* Cambridge: Cambridge University Press, 1996.

Macquarrie, John. *Mary for All Christians.* London: Collins, 1991.

Maisch, Ingrid. *Maria Magdalena zwischen Verachtung und Verehrung: Das Bild einer Frau im Spiegel der Jahrhunderte.* Freiburg im Breisgau: Herder, 1996. English translation: *Mary Magdalene: The Image of a Woman through the Centuries.* Translated by Linda M. Maloney. Collegeville, Minn.: Liturgical Press, 1998.

Marjanen, Antti. *The Woman Jesus Loved: Mary Magdalene in the Nag Hammadi Library and Related Documents.* Nag Hammadi and Manichaean Studies 40. Leiden: Brill, 1996.

Marmardji, A. S., ed. *Diatessaron de Tatien: Texte arabe établi, traduit en français, collationné avec les anciennes versions syriaques, suivi d'un évangéliaire diatessarique syriaque et accompagné de quatre plances hors texte.* Beirut: Imprimerie catholique, 1935.

Masson, Charles. "Le tombeau vide." *RTP* 32 (1944): 161–74.

McCarthy, Carmel, trans. *Saint Ephrem's Commentary on the Diatessaron.* Oxford: Oxford University Press, 1993.

Ménard, Jacques-É. *L'Évangile selon Thomas.* NHS 5. Leiden: Brill, 1975.

Metzger, Bruce M. *The Early Versions of the New Testament: Their Origin, Transmission, and Limitations.* Oxford: Clarendon, 1977.

Meyer, Marvin W. "Making Mary Male: The Categories 'Male' and 'Female' in the Gospel of Thomas." *NTS* 31 (1985): 554–70.

———, trans. with introduction. *The Gospel of Thomas: The Hidden Sayings of Jesus.* Interpreted by Harold Bloom. New York: HarperSan-Francisco, 1992.

Meynet, Roland. *L'Évangile selon Saint Luc: Analyse rhétorique.* 2 vols. Paris: Cerf, 1988.

Mimouni, Simon C. *Dormition et assomption de Marie: Histoire des traditions anciennes.* ThH 98. Paris: Beauchesne, 1995.

Mohri, Erika. *Maria Magdalena: Frauenbilder in Evangelientexten des 1. bis 3. Jahrhunderts.* Marburg: Elwert, 2000.

Moltmann-Wendel, Elisabeth. *The Women around Jesus.* New York: Crossroad, 1982.

Morard, Françoise. "Un évangile écrit par une femme?" *Bulletin du Centre Protestant d'Études* 49 (May 1997): 27–34.

Murray, Robert. *Symbols of Church and Kingdom: A Study in Early Syriac Tradition.* Cambridge: Cambridge University Press, 1975.

Norelli, Enrico. *Ascension du prophète Isaïe.* Apocryphes. Turnhout: Brepols, 1993.

———. *L'Ascensione di Isaia: Studi su un apocrifo al crocevia dei cristianesimi.* Origini NS 1. Bologna: Dehoniane, 1994.

Nürnberg, Rosemarie. "Apostolae Apostolorum: Die Frauen am Grab als erste Zeuginnen der Auferstehung in der Väterexegese." Pages 228–42 in *Stimuli, Exegese und ihre Hermeneutik in Antike und Christentum: Festschrift Ernst Dassmann.* JAC.E 23. Münster: Aschendorff, 1996.

O'Collins, Gerald, and Daniel Kendall. "Mary Magdalene As Major Witness to Jesus' Resurrection." *TS* 48 (1987): 631–46.

Pagels, Elaine. *The Gnostic Gospels.* New York: Random House, 1981.

———. "Visions, Appearances, and Apostolic Authority: Gnostic and Orthodox Traditions." Pages 415–30 in *Gnosis: Festschrift für Hans Jonas.* Edited by Barbara Aland. Göttingen: Vandenhoeck & Ruprecht, 1978.

Parrott, Douglas M. "Gnostic and Orthodox Disciples in the Second and Third Centuries." Pages 193–219 in *Nag Hammadi, Gnosticism, and Early Christianity.* Edited by Charles W. Hedrick and Robert Hodgson Jr. Peabody, Mass.: Hendrickson, 1986.

Parsons, P. J. "3525: Gospel of Mary." Pages 12–14 in vol. 50 of *The Oxyrhynchus Papyri.* London: Egypt Exploration Society, 1983.

Parvey, Constance F. "The Theology and Leadership of Women in the New Testament." Pages 139–49 in *Religion and Sexism.* Edited by Rosemary Radford Ruether. New York: Simon & Schuster, 1974.

Pasquier, Anne. *L'Évangile selon Marie*. BCNH.T 10. Québec: Les presses de l'Université Laval, 1983.

Pelikan, Jaroslav. *Mary through the Centuries*. New Haven: Yale University Press, 1996.

Perkins, Pheme. *The Gnostic Dialogue: The Early Church and the Crisis of Gnosticism*. Theological Inquiries: Studies in Contemporary Biblical and Theological Problems. New York: Paulist, 1980.

————. "Gospel of Mary." *ABD* 4:583–84.

————. "Gospel of Thomas." Pages 535–60 in vol. 2 of *Searching the Scriptures*. Edited by Elisabeth Schüssler Fiorenza. 2 vols. New York: Crossroad, 1993–94.

————. *Peter: Apostle for the Whole Church*. Columbia: University of South Carolina Press, 1994.

Petersen, Silke. *"Zerstört die Werke der Weiblichkeit!" Maria Magdalena, Salome und andere Jüngerinnen Jesu in christlich-gnostischen Schriften*. Nag Hammadi and Manichaean Studies 48. Leiden: Brill, 1999.

Petersen, William L. *The Diatessaron and Ephrem Syrus As Sources of Romanos the Melodist*. CSCO 475, CSCO.Sub 74. Leuven: Peeters, 1985.

————. "The Diatessaron of Tatian." Pages 77–96 in *The Text of the New Testament in Contemporary Research: Essays on the* Status Quaestionis. Edited by Bart D. Ehrman and Michael W. Holmes. Grand Rapids: Eerdmans, 1995.

————. *Tatian's Diatessaron: Its Creation, Dissemination, Significance, and History in Scholarship*. Supplements to Vigiliae christianae 25. Leiden: Brill, 1994.

Price, Robert M. "Mary Magdalene: Gnostic Apostle?" *Grail* 6 (1990): 54–76.

Puech, Henri-Charles. "Gnostische Evangelien und verwandte Dokumente." Pages 285–329 in vol. 1 of *Neutestamentliche Apokryphen in deutscher Übersetzung*. Edited by Edgar Hennecke and Wilhelm Schneemelcher. 2 vols. Tübingen: Mohr Siebeck, 1959–64.

Puech, Henri-Charles, and Beate Blatz. "The Gospel of Mary." Pages 391–95 in vol. 1 of *New Testament Apocrypha*. Edited by Wilhelm Schneemelcher. Translated by R. McL. Wilson. 2 vols. Rev. ed. Cambridge: Clarke; Louisville: Westminster John Knox, 1991–92.

Revillout, Eugène, ed. *Évangile des douze apôtres*. PO 2.2. Paris: Librairie de Paris/Firmin-Didot et Cie, 1907.

Ricci, Carla. *Mary Magdalene and Many Others: Women Who Followed Jesus*. Translated by Paul Burns. Minneapolis: Fortress, 1994.

Roberts, C. H. "463: The Gospel of Mary." Pages 18–23 in vol. 3 of *Catalogue of the Greek Papyri in the John Rylands Library*. 4 vols. Manchester: Manchester University Press, 1911–52.

Robinson, James M., ed. *The Nag Hammadi Library in English*. 4th rev. ed.
    Leiden: Brill, 1996.
Rossi, Mary Ann. "Priesthood, Precedent, and Prejudice: On Recovering the
    Women Priests of Early Christianity." *JFSR* 7 (1991): 73–93.
Ruether, Rosemary Radford. *Mary: The Feminine Face of the Church*.
    Philadelphia: Westminster, 1977.
Ruschmann, Susanne. *Maria von Magdala im Johannesevangelium:
    Jüngerin—Zeugin—Lebensbotin*. NTAbh 40. Münster: Aschendorff, 2002.
Schaberg, Jane. "How Mary Magdalene Became a Whore: Mary Magdalene
    Is in Fact the Primary Witness to the Fundamental Data of Early Chris-
    tian Faith." *BRev* 8 (1992): 30–37, 51–52.
———. *The Resurrection of Mary Magdalene: Legends, Apocrypha, and the
    Christian Testament*. New York: Continuum, 2002.
———. "Thinking Back through the Magdalene." *Continuum* 1.2 (1991):
    71–90.
Schenke, Hans-Martin. "Bemerkungen zum koptischen Papyrus Berolinen-
    sis 8502." Pages 315–22 in *Festschrift zum 150 jährigen Bestehen des
    Berliner Ägyptischen Museums*. Mitteilungen aus der ägyptischen
    Sammlung 8. Berlin: Akademie, 1974.
Schillebeeckx, Edward, and Catharina Halkes. *Mary: Yesterday, Today,
    Tomorrow*. London: SCM, 1993.
Schmid, Renate. *Maria Magdalena in gnostischen Schriften*. Material-Edition
    29. Munich: Arbeitsgemeinschaft für Religions- und Weltanschauungs-
    fragen, 1990.
Schmidt, Carl. *Gnostiche Schriften in koptischer Sprache aus dem Codex
    Brucianus*. TU 8.1. Leipzig: Hinrichs, 1892.
———. *Koptisch-gnostische Schriften*. Vol. 1. 4th ed. GCS 45. Berlin:
    Akademie, 1981.
———. *Pistis Sophia: Ein gnostisches Originalwerk des 3. Jahrhunderts aus
    dem Koptischen übersetzt*. Leipzig: Hinrichs, 1925.
———. "Die Urschrift der Pistis Sophia." *ZNW* 24 (1925): 218–40.
———. "Ein vorirenäisches gnostisches Originalwerk in koptischer
    Sprache." *SPAW.PH* 36 (1896): 839–47.
———, ed. *Pistis Sophia*. Translation and notes by Violet MacDermot. NHS
    9. Leiden: Brill, 1978.
Schneemelcher, Wilhelm, ed. *New Testament Apocrypha*. Translated by
    R. McL. Wilson. 2 vols. Rev. ed. Cambridge: Clarke; Louisville: West-
    minster John Knox, 1991–92.
Schottroff, Luise. "Maria Magdalena und die Frauen am Grabe Jesu." *EvT*
    42 (1982): 3–25.
Schottroff, Luise, Silvia Schroer, and Marie-Theres Wacker. *Feminist Inter-
    pretation: The Bible in Women's Perspective*. Translated by Martin and
    Barbara Rumscheidt. Minneapolis: Fortress, 1998.

Schüssler Fiorenza, Elisabeth. *Bread Not Stone: The Challenge of Feminist Biblical Interpretation*. Boston: Beacon, 1984.

—. *In Memory of Her: A Feminist Theological Reconstruction of Christian Origins*. New York: Crossroad, 1983.

—. *Jesus, Miriam's Child, Sophia's Prophet: Critical Issues in Feminist Christology*. New York: Continuum, 1994.

—. "Mary Magdalene: Apostle to the Apostles." *Union Theological Seminary Journal* (April 1975): 22–24.

—, ed. *Searching the Scriptures*. 2 vols. New York: Crossroad, 1993–94.

Scopello, Maddalena. "Marie-Madeleine et la tour: Pistis et sophia." Pages 179–96 in *Figures du Nouveau Testament chez les Pères*. CBiPa 3. Strasbourg: Centre d'analyse et de documentation patristiques, 1991.

Sellew, Philip. "An Early Coptic Witness to the *Dormitio Mariae* at Yale: P.CtYBR inv. 1788 Revisited." *BASP* 37 (2000): 37–69.

Setzer, Claudia. "Excellent Women: Female Witness to the Resurrection." *JBL* 116 (1997): 259–72.

Shoemaker, Stephen J. *The Ancient Traditions of the Virgin Mary's Dormition and Assumption*. Oxford Early Christian Studies. Oxford: Clarendon, forthcoming.

—. "Mary and the Discourse of Orthodoxy: Early Christian Identity and the Ancient Dormition Legends." Ph.D. diss., Duke University, 1997.

—. "Rethinking the 'Gnostic Mary': Mary of Nazareth and Mary of Magdala in Early Christian Tradition." *JECS* 9 (2001): 555–95.

Smith Lewis, Agnes. *The Old Syriac Gospels or Evangelion da-mepharreshe*. London: Williams & Norgate, 1910.

Strycker, Émile de. *La forme la plus ancienne du Protévangile de Jacques*. SHG 33. Brussels: Société des Bollandistes, 1961.

Synek, Eva M. "'Die andere Maria': Zum Bild der Maria von Magdala in den östlichen Kirchentraditionen." *OrChr* 79 (1995): 181–96.

Tardieu, Michel. *Écrits gnostiques: Codex de Berlin*. Sources gnostiques et manichéennes 1. Paris: Cerf, 1984.

Tardieu, Michel, and Jean-Daniel Dubois. *Introduction à la littérature gnostique I*. Paris: Cerf and CNRS, 1986.

Thimmes, Pamela. "Memory and Re-vision: Mary Magdalene Research since 1975." *CurBS* 6 (1998): 193–226.

Thompson, Mary R. *Mary of Magdala: Apostle and Leader*. New York and Mahwah, N.J.: Paulist, 1995.

Till, Walter C., and Hans-Martin Schenke. *Die gnostischen Schriften des koptischen Papyrus Berolinensis 8502*. TU 60. Berlin: Akademie, 1972.

Torjesen, Karen Jo. *When Women Were Priests: Women's Leadership in the Early Church and the Scandal of Their Subordination in the Rise of Christianity*. San Francisco: Harper, 1993.

Vööbus, Arthur. *Early Versions of the New Testament: Manuscript Studies.* PETSE 6. Stockholm: Estonian Theological Society in Exile, 1954.

———, ed. *Didascalia Apostolorum in Syriac.* CSCO 401–402, 407–408. Louvain: Secretariat du CorpusSCO, 1979.

Warner, Marina. *Alone of All Her Sex: The Myth and Cult of the Virgin Mary.* London: Weidenfeld & Nicolson, 1976.

Williams, Michael Allen. *Rethinking "Gnosticism": An Argument for Dismantling a Dubious Category.* Princeton, N.J.: Princeton University Press, 1996.

Wilson, Robert McL. "The New Testament in the Gnostic Gospel of Mary." *NTS* 3 (1956–57): 236–43.

Wilson, Robert McL., and George W. MacRae. "BG,1: The Gospel according to Mary." Pages 453–71 in *Nag Hammadi Codices V,2–5 and VI with Papyrus Berolinensis 8502,1 and 4.* Edited by Douglas M. Parrott. NHS 11. Leiden: Brill, 1979.

Witherington, Ben. "On the Road with Mary Magdalene, Joanna, Susanna, and Other Disciples—Luke 8:1–3." *ZNW* 70 (1979): 243–48.

Wright, William. *Apocryphal Acts of the Apostles: Syriac and English.* 2 vols. London and Edinburgh: Williams & Norgate, 1871.

———. *Contributions to the Apocryphal Literature.* London: Williams & Norgate, 1865.

Zervos, George T. "Dating the Protevangelium of James: The Justin Martyr Connection." Pages 415–34 in *SBL Seminar Papers, 1994.* SBLSP 33. Atlanta: Scholars Press, 1994.

———. "An Early Non-canonical Annunciation Story." Pages 664–91 in *SBL Seminar Papers, 1997.* SBLSP 36. Atlanta: Scholars Press, 1997.

———. "Prolegomena to a Critical Edition of the *Genesis Marias* (*Protevangelium Jacobi*): The Greek Manuscripts." Ph.D. diss., Duke University, 1986.

Index of Primary Sources

Hebrew Bible

Hebrew and Jewish Writings

New Testament

Early Christian Writings

Greek Sources

Index of Modern Authors